The Lakeland Ridges Challenge Walk

TOM CALVERT

Leading Edge™
press and publishing

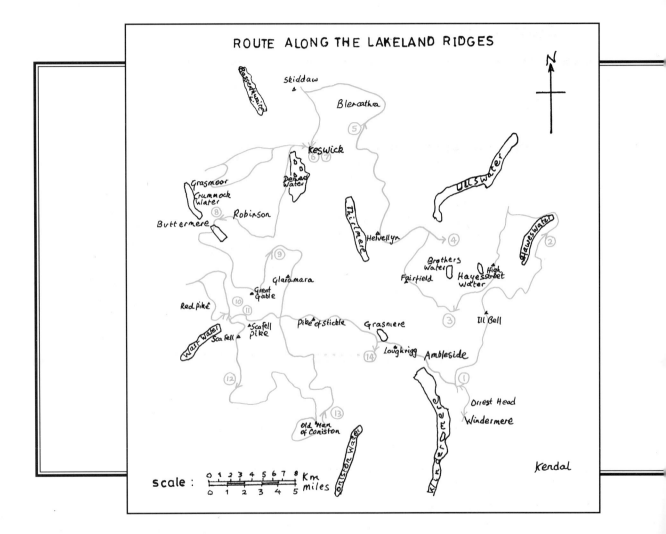

Contents

In memory of Emily and Marion Stell, who inspired me to travel

Published by Leading Edge Press & Publishing Ltd

The Old Chapel, Burtersett, Hawes, North Yorkshire DL8 3PB. Tel 01969 667566 Fax 01969 667788

© **Text & photographs:** Tom Calvert 1995
© **Maps:** Harvey Map Services Ltd
© **Page designs:** Leading Edge Press & Publishing

A CIP Catalogue record for this book is available from the British Library.

ISBN 0-948135-56-5

Designed by Jon Smith, using QuarkXpress 3.3 on Power Macintosh 7100
Additional editorial work by Stan Abbott and Paddy Dillon
Printed and bound by: Ebenezer Baylis & Son Ltd, Worcester

Compass bearings shown in the viewpoint graphics in this book are from magnetic north, estimated by the Ordnance Survey at the time of going to press to be approximately 5° west of grid north.
Compass bearings in respect of the viewpoint diagrams only have therefore been measured from grid north plus 5°. Distances are 'as the crow flies'. Heights in metres are based on Harvey's maps.

Rights of Way: Readers/walkers are reminded that they may be crossing land in private ownership. Sections of the walk on high fell ground are not shown as public paths on the definitive map and the writer cannot guarantee that public rights of way exist throughout this walk. Where necessary, the permission of land owners must be sought and walkers should, of course, respect the rights and property of others at all times.

Warning: Walking over the fells can be dangerous. While every care has been given to the compilation of the walk route description, walkers follow the route at their own risk. Neither the author nor the publisher shall be held in any way responsible for any injury, damage or death befalling any participant in the walk.

■ *The front cover photograph shows the author on Catbells above Derwentwater*

The idea

MANY years ago, the late W A Poucher described a series of ridge walks in the Lake District in his book, *Over Lakeland Fells*[1]. In it, he said he thought it would be impossible to traverse all the ridges described in a single journey undertaken over a normal holiday period.

This book, however, describes a series of ridge traverses compiled into one journey, and is proof that the majority of the Lakeland country can be covered in a fortnight's holiday. The extended ridge walk was completed in a 15-day period during May and June, and involved ascending and descending all the major Lakeland peaks and ridges, covering a distance of more than 180 miles (290 km), with more than 18,000m (59,500ft) of ascent and descent.

The writer's intricate knowledge of the Lake District has developed from an early childhood spent on its northern periphery and initial schooldays in the heart of the area. Subsequently, many happy days have been spent walking and climbing in the district with friends and mountaineering club members. The idea of creating a Lakeland Ridges Challenge Walk has been a long-held ambition.

To have an idea is one thing, to put it into practice quite another. Often "*Walter Mitty*" pipe-dreams are not at all feasible. Detailed analysis and feasibility study were essential. Knowledge of the Lake District helped to decide where the journey should start, the course it should take, and its breakdown into practical sections coinciding with suitable locations for overnight accommodation. I decided against the purist's idea of being more or less self-sufficient throughout the expedition. The burden of camping at the end of a strenuous day was somewhat off-putting, and I also considered that meeting like-minded people during overnight stops would be mentally stimulating. Many hours perusing maps eventually resulted in a complete route divided into sections which would provide the best chance of success. The start and finishing point was Windermere, with the advantage of easy access by car, train or bus.

This book explains the origins of the idea, preparations for its implementation, its undertaking and completion, together with historical, topical and other digressions. Maps and photographs illustrate the many varied and beautiful aspects of the route.

Some readers may wish to follow the journey in its entirety or in parts. Others may feel satisfied by remaining within the comfort of an armchair and completing an imaginary journey over the peaks and along the ridges. Whichever method is adopted, it is hoped that the reader will absorb the history and scenic beauty of what is still a magical and treasured part of Britain.

■ *Maps in this book are based on Harvey's walkers' maps, and spellings of place names in the text follow Harvey's usage. Readers using Ordnance Survey or other maps will notice some minor differences (Bow Fell for Bowfell, for example, Sca Fell for Scafell and Hawse for Hause). Where these may lead to confusion, the alternative spellings have been given in italicised brackets after the name.*

[1] *Over Lakeland Fells*; W A Poucher; Chapman & Hall 1948

Prologue

IT was refreshing to leave the slight stuffiness of the train that had taken me from the main line station at Oxenholme, near Kendal, along the single-track branch line to Windermere.

My rucksack weighed heavily as I alighted from the train and walked away from the station. A group of children passed me, chattering excitedly on their way home from school. I recalled my happy years at Huyton Hill School, near Pull Wyke Bay, on the north-west shore of Windermere, from where we used to walk out, crocodile-style, along the lanes and into the beautiful Lakeland countryside.

Climbing through the woods above Old Elleray to Orrest Head my spirits rose as I absorbed the aroma from the flowers and the shrubs.

The panorama from Orrest Head was resplendent but a little challenging as I realised that the peaks and ridges in view would have to be conquered during the next 14 days. There were proposals to put a memorial to the late Alfred Wainwright here, but these have now been abandoned amid some controversy.

At Windermere Youth Hostel I enjoyed the sense of community and admired the adventurous spirit of young visitors who had come from far away to this corner of England.

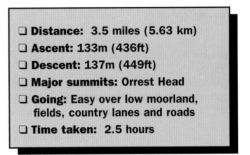

- **Distance:** 3.5 miles (5.63 km)
- **Ascent:** 133m (436ft)
- **Descent:** 137m (449ft)
- **Major summits:** Orrest Head
- **Going:** Easy over low moorland, fields, country lanes and roads
- **Time taken:** 2.5 hours

1 WINDERMERE is the frenetic hub of the tourist industry in the Lake District, and for this reason those who prefer quieter environs may be anxious not to linger. Others may wish to enjoy the hectic holiday atmosphere before entering the more tranquil environment of the hills.

After leaving the station, the route takes you past the tourist information office, then across the A591 to the entrance to a driveway, where a large sign fixed to a wall points the way to Orrest Head.

The road and path weave their way up the hillside through mixed woodland with rhododendrons, above Old Elleray, until you reach a path running at right-angles. Turn right to a metal kissing gate, beyond which it is only a short distance to the viewpoint at **Orrest Head** (238m/781ft).

Here, just three-quarters of a mile from Windermere station, is a reward that should not be missed… a mag-

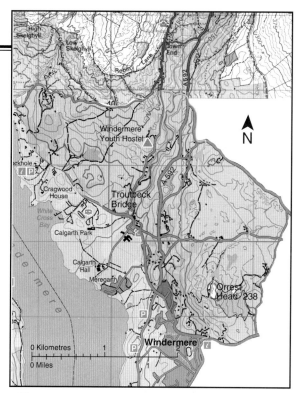

nificent panoramic view of Lake Windermere with the Langdale fells beyond, as well as the fells around Coniston Water to the west — a sight of real encouragement and motivation.

2 FROM Orrest Head follow the footpath in a north-easterly direction to The Causeway Farm and then go north-east along the minor road to Near Orrest. Take the footpath to Far Orrest and then to the Moorhowe Road at Fusethwaite Yeat. From here follow the road north which descends to the A592 Patterdale to Windermere road. On reaching this road turn north for approximately 80 yards (75m) where access can be gained to a footpath leading to a footbridge over Trout Beck. Continue up from the west side of the beck to the road between Troutbeck Bridge and Town End. At the road turn left (south) for Windermere Youth Hostel at High Cross Castle, or right (north) for Town End and Troutbeck village if accommodation has been arranged here.

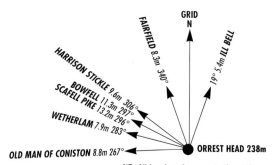

NB: All bearings from magnetic north

3 THE youth hostel is an interesting building and its pleasant grounds, with rhododendron-lined driveway, were once more extensive. The original country residence was formerly a grandiose wooden property, partially roofed in glass, but it was gutted by fire in 1915. The present building is of much sturdier construction, in concrete and stone and once boasted a turreted tower, subsequently removed.

■ *Windermere and Langdale Pikes from Orrest Head*

DAY 1: Windermere to Haweswater

THE short hike from Windermere station had been a stroll compared with what lay before me as dawn brought clear, bright skies with only the odd cumulus cloud. Good weather on the first day of any adventure boosts the morale, and I was excited, yet slightly apprehensive.

My first day's real journey would lead me from the hubbub of the Windermere area, to bring me a fleeting acquaintance with four ancient trading routes and steep me in nostalgia for the communities submerged beneath Haweswater in the name of quenching the thirst of industrial Manchester. But it was to be by the shores of this artificially enlarged lake that my day would find its highlight — a highlight brought to me courtesy of wild Nature that still characterises much of the eastern part of the Lake District.

The prelude to this fine finale to the day was continuing excellent weather, although the haze grew in intensity as the day wore on. Having left the youth hostel before nine, I took an early lunch at the summit of Ill Bell, shortly before noon, where the visibility remained good enough to identify some of Lakeland's major peaks all around me. It was nice to find some respite from the busy traffic of Saturday walkers as I skirted High Street in fine weather at the summit of Mardale Ill Bell.

- **Distance:** 14 miles (22.5 km)
- **Ascent:** 1,072m (3,517ft)
- **Descent:** 948m (3,110ft)
- **Major summits:** Yoke, Ill Bell, Froswick, Mardale Ill Bell, Harter Fell, Branstree (Artlecrag Pike), Selside Pike
- **Going:** Moderately strenuous over passes and undulating ridges
- **Time taken:** 9 hours

By Harter Fell, at two o' clock, I was beginning to feel confident that I would be able to accomplish the day's schedule more easily than anticipated, although I confess to flagging a little on the climb up Branstree an hour later.

But it was on the last leg of the walk, as I approached Haweswater Hotel, that my day was made when I came upon a couple staring intently skyward through binoculars. They told me the eagles at nearby Riggindale had raised two chicks this year, although one was considerably stronger than the other.

I joined them to gaze into the sky above Mardale Common and suddenly caught a glimpse of a bird of

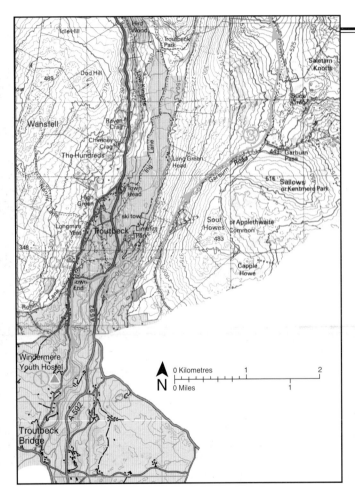

prey soaring very high, some 3-4,000ft up. From behind a bank of cloud the other parent bird flew into the late afternoon sunshine. I had seen the eagles of Riggindale! It was a magnificent sight, and I considered myself blessed to be the recipient of such a marvellous spectacle.

❶ FROM Windermere Youth Hostel, take the ascending road to Town End. Here you pass the 17th century farmhouse and spinning gallery, formerly owned by the Browne family who were long-established sheep farmers until 1944, when the farm was acquired by the National Trust. Now it contains carved woodwork, books, papers, furniture, and a fascinating collection of bygone implements assembled by the Browne family.

At Troutbeck post office, take the road to the right (east) which descends to Troutbeck Bridge and Troutbeck Parish Church, with its 18th century bell-tower and large and colourful east window designed by Sir Edward Burne-Jones. The window depicts the crucifixion, with a youthful, unbearded Jesus and — unusually — it is to Jesus that the church is dedicated. One story has it that Burne-Jones was assisted in his work on the window by two other pre-Raphaelite artists, William Morris and Ford Maddox Brown. The churchyard, with its yew

■ *The track to Garburn Road and Pass, Yoke, Ill Bell and Froswick from Troutbeck*

■ *Haweswater from Little Harter Fell*

trees and three lychgates, is at its best in the spring when the azaleas and rhododendrons are in flower, creating a colourful vista and delightful aroma.

❷ FROM the church turn south and walk along the footpath on the west side of the A592 road for 140 yards (125m), using the pedestrian way by the side of the narrow bridge over Trout Beck to avoid possible danger from fast-moving traffic.

A walled lane leads up the hillside and shortly joins the Garburn Road, an ancient drove road to Kentmere, that was once part of a cross-country highway of some importance.

3 AT the summit of Garburn Pass, take the well-marked track in a northerly direction. There is undulating ground, boggy in places, to cross in the early stages where the track follows a stone wall on its gradual ascent to the summit of **Yoke** (706m/2,316ft).

From here a well-marked path, parts of which are suffering severe erosion, leads to **Ill Bell** (757m/2,484 ft). On a clear day, Ill Bell rewards the walker with a fine panorama: to the west are Scafell (*Sca Fell*), Scafell Pike, Great Gable, Bowfell (*Bow Fell*), Crinkle Crags and Harrison Stickle. Northwards, and closer, are Fairfield, Helvellyn, St Sunday Crag, Thornthwaite Crag, High Street, Mardale Ill Bell, and Harter Fell.

4 THE summit of Ill Bell is the highest point on this section of ridge and has a large cairn perched on its rocky top. There are crags to the north-east and east, and therefore care should be taken when leaving the summit to follow the undulating path which goes north-west for about 430 yards (400m) before heading due north over **Froswick** (720m/2,359 ft). Heavy use has unfortunately made the path very wide in places, as you head towards High Street, briefly joining the old Roman Road, before skirting east-northeast around Hall Cove, above Gavel Crag and Bleathwaite Crag, to reach **Mardale Ill Bell** (761m/2,497ft). This next summit enjoys a fine vantage at the head of the Haweswater valley, commanding excellent views of the surrounding fells.

5 THERE is an easy descent in a south-easterly direction from the summit to the head of Nan Bield Pass, where there is a large cairn and shelter. This gracefully

engineered pass, with its curves and zig-zags, was once the main trade thoroughfare between Kentmere and Mardale.

Nan Bield Pass is crossed at right angles to commence the short but steep ascent to the summit plateau of **Harter Fell** (778m/2,552ft). The summit itself is recognisable by its stone cairn, into which have been inserted rusty old fence stakes.

6 THE well-known view of Haweswater is from the cairn at the eastern end of the summit ridge, and is both recommended and poignant. The water level was raised after the original lake and its catchment area had

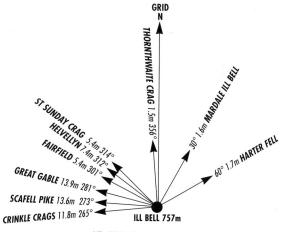

NB: All bearings from magnetic north

been purchased by Manchester Corporation by means of an Act of Parliament in 1919. Work was started on the construction of the necessary dam at the northern end of the lake but the arrival of the depression in the 1930s meant that it was not finally completed until 1941. The rise in the water level drowned the little village of Mardale Green, the ghostly rubble of whose remains emerge occasionally from the waters in years of severe drought, most recently in 1984.

Once Mardale Green boasted a pub, the Dun Bull, and a church, Holy Trinity. Alas, the church and the tall yew trees that surrounded it are no more. A final service was held in 1935 before it was demolished and its stone used in the construction of the reservoir. The church furnishings were despatched to new homes in other churches in the area (the pulpit to Borrowdale, the weather vane to Shap). The coffins were exhumed from the churchyard for reburial at Shap, recalling the days before 1728 when the dead of Mardale used to be carried on horseback to the same destination.

Local lore tells of people who have heard the uncanny peeling of the bell from the vicinity of the old church. The story of life in old Mardale is told in an interesting little book by David and Joan Hay[2].

At the eastern end of the summit ridge care is required, especially in mist or inclement weather, as below the cairn at this point there are crags which must be avoided. The track to follow is the one turning almost 90° from the summit ridge to follow a fence line in a south-easterly direction.

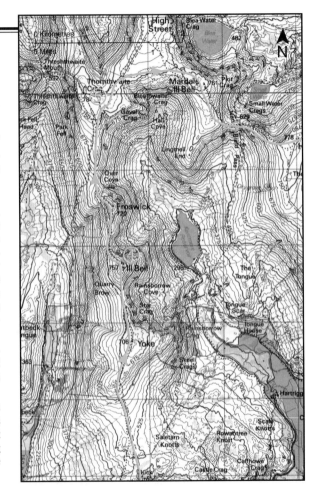

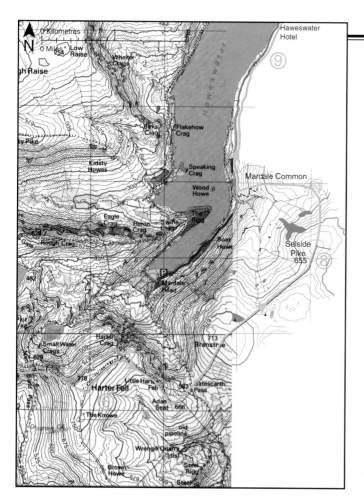

The descent is gradual. However, before it begins in earnest, it is worth making a slight detour to the right to ascend the lesser summit of **Adam Seat** (666m/2,185ft). This is a good place from which to gaze down Longsleddale, one of the less frequented Lakeland valleys, whose charm remains relatively undisturbed as a result.

Like Nan Bield, Gatescarth Pass is again crossed at right angles at its head. Gatescarth Pass is on the old packhorse route connecting Longsleddale and Mardale. This route went on to serve the huge slate quarry at Wren Gill, which was in production for two centuries, being operated most recently by Italian prisoners during the last war.

7 THE ascent to the summit of **Branstree** (713m/2,339ft) – a name not shown on some maps and given on the latest 1:25000 Ordnance Survey map as Artlecrag Pike – is easy, following an old wire fence in a north-easterly direction.

The summit is marked by a rather unusual Ordnance Survey trig point, consisting of a circular bronze disc, set in concrete, rather than the ubiquitous concrete pillar.

Continuing in a north-easterly direction, the

2 _Mardale, The Drowned Village,_ David & Joan Hay, Friends of the Lake District, 1976

next stretch of fell to Selside Pike consists of easy but featureless terrain, the only object of interest being a stone pillar constructed as a survey sight post during the building of the aqueduct from Haweswater to the Watchgate water treatment plant, near Kendal. This relic (Grid ref: NY 483102) remains as a memorial to the former feats of engineering.

On a clear day, **Selside Pike** (655m/2,149ft) is a good point from which to view the northern end of the Pennine ridge, including its highest point – Cross Fell (893m/2,930ft) – and the Eden Valley below its western flanks.

8 FROM Selside Pike, a short and relatively steep descent takes the walker in a northerly direction to the Old Corpse Road, over which — as previously mentioned — the inhabitants of Mardale carried their dead to Shap for burial until the churchyard at Mardale (originally a chapel of ease for Shap Abbey) was consecrated as a burial ground and the church given rights for the conduct of baptisms and weddings.

Descending westward on the Old Corpse Road provides fine views of Mardale Ill Bell, High Street, and Riggindale where eagles have returned to breed for a number of years now. Just before the sharp descent to the road along the eastern shore of Haweswater are the remains of a number of buildings — a stark reminder that you are entering a dale which had been inhabited for centuries but, because of our growing need for water, is now little more than a ghost valley.

9 THE route follows the road to the right (north) for a little over a mile and quarter (2 km) to the Haweswater Hotel, where accommodation may be available. Alternatively, it is just over another two and a quarter miles (3.6 km) to the hamlet of Burnbanks, established during the construction of Haweswater dam and now housing water services maintenance staff. Nearby farms, Naddle and Thornthwaite Hall provide bed and breakfast.

The hamlet is reached by leaving the road at Naddle Bridge, for a short but delightful walk through woodland which, in late spring, has a carpet of bluebells. This path forms part of the well-known Coast to Coast Walk devised by the late Alfred Wainwright.

■ *Boundary marker on Adam Seat, looking towards Branstree (Artlecrag Pike)*

■ *Above: Mardale III Bell, High Street and Small Water from Harter Fell*

■ *Left: Survey pillar near Branstree (Artlecrag Pike)*

■ *Haweswater and Harter Fell from above Burnbanks*

DAY 2: Haweswater to Kirkstone Pass

ANOTHER fine day with clear skies but considerable haze, even in the early morning. I walked from the Haweswater Hotel to the edge of the reservoir. It was perfectly still, and the tranquillity moved me, making me realise that the early morning of any day should be savoured for its stillness and serenity. Birds in the bluebell-bedecked woods by the water's edge were busy with their morning chorus as I gazed up to the head of the reservoir, with Mardale Ill Bell and Harter Fell framing the scene. The odd pied wagtail darted along the shoreline rocks, carrion crows above gave their sharp 'kar kar' cry, woodpigeons flew hurriedly from nocturnal perches, and I could hear a willow-warbler.

The hawthorn blossom was nearly at its peak and its sweet aroma hinted at the summer to come. Ash trees had broken bud and were coming into leaf. The hillside streams, discharging to the reservoir, were now reduced to a trickle following three weeks of relatively dry weather. I hoped that this would continue a little longer, as often when the weather changes in Lakeland it remains unsettled for some time.

The day began with a circuit of the eastern end of Haweswater, followed by a climb up towards High Street before I stopped for a rest and food beside the small cairn marking the summit of Wether Hill. Gazing along the old Roman road inevitably brought back memories of my old walking colleague Peter, who died in 1984 at the tragically early age of 47 and whose remains now rest in the church-

> ❏ **Distance:** 14.25 miles (22.93 km)
> ❏ **Ascent:** 1,104m (3,327ft)
> ❏ **Descent:** 818m (2,684ft)
> ❏ **Major summits:** Wether Hill, High Raise, Kidsty Pike, High Street, Stony Cove Pike, Caudale Moor
> ❏ **Going:** Mildly strenuous with some scrambling over broad extensive ridges on mainly well-defined paths, boggy in places
> ❏ **Time taken:** 9 hours

yard at Seathwaite. Peter was a fellow student at Newton Rigg college in the 1960s who used to follow the harriers and hounds across the fells. He also appeared to have psychic abilities and now I recalled a tale he told me of a time he had been suddenly confronted on High Street by the ghostly apparition of a Roman centurion in full dress.

I had been on High Street many times — once with Peter walking its entire 15 miles from near Penrith to Troutbeck — and I had always been dogged by rain, snow, hail, wind, low cloud and mist. Today, however, it looked as though I should make the summit in relatively clear conditions, and indeed by the time I got there the hills were basking in sunshine — but not a centurion to be seen!

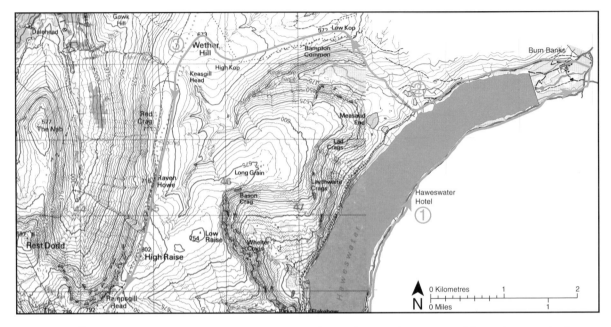

① IF you have stayed overnight at the Haweswater Hotel, you will find the walk along the road above the eastern shore of the lake to Burnbanks a pleasant one. At various points streams from the wooded fellside cascade into road culverts which in turn discharge into the lake. The trees above the road are a haven for a variety of wild birds and their singing soothes as well as stimulates the mind, giving exhilarating pleasure in the early morning.

After passing the dam, the road passes old parkland dotted with gnarled oaks, the remnants, probably, of a former hunting forest. At Naddle Bridge you climb over a stile to join the route of the Coast to Coast Walk, which passes through delightful woodland to the hamlet of Burnbanks. From here the Coast to Coast route is followed in a westerly direction, along the side of Haweswater for about a mile and a quarter (2 km) to Measand Beck.

② JUST past the bridge crossing the beck there is an attractive viewpoint of the lake towards its head below Mardale Ill Bell and Harter Fell. Although maps show a footpath up the south-west side of Measand

■ *Above: Kirkstone Pass and Brothers Water*
■ *Right: The Forces on Measand Beck*

Beck, it is better to follow the track up the north-east side which passes a series of waterfalls known as The Forces, popular for picnic parties. Further upstream, you pass by a footbridge and follow a fairly indistinct path heading north-west up the slopes of **Low Kop** (572m/1,875ft). After this the gradient eases, and a gently-sloping fell with springy turf leads west to **High Kop** (664m/2,179ft). From here continue north-west to a small cairn on the top of **Wether Hill** (673m/2,208ft) near the Roman road on the main ridge to High Street.

❸ HERE, if the day is clear, a diversion north to **Loadpot Hill** (671m/2201ft) offers views of the eastern end of Ullswater, Howtown and Pooley Bridge. Otherwise, you follow the Roman road south-south-west over **Red Crag** (711m/2,333ft) and **High Raise** (802m/2,634ft).

A slight detour at Rampsgill Head gives excellent views of the Martindale valley. Another slight diversion south-east for about 500 yards (450m) will let you take in **Kidsty Pike** (780m/2,560ft). This summit, on a clear day, provides excellent views of the head of Haweswater and the crags above Riggindale, on its south side frequented by eagles. Returning north-west one rejoins the Roman road to the Straits of Riggindale.

From here the track rises slowly to **High Street** (828m/2,718ft) by a broad and in places somewhat eroded path. The actual Roman road passes the summit at a lower level on its west side. Roman engineers preferred a straight line wherever possible: not surprising, really, as this road was probably built to carry infantry

from Galava, near Ambleside, to the Brocavum fort on the site of which now stands Brougham Castle, on the River Eamont near Penrith.

❹ FROM the summit of High Street, also known as Racecourse Hill on account of races that have taken place there in the past, there is an overwhelming panoramic view of all Lakeland's eastern fells. On a cold blustery day in winter, however, it is not the place to hang about, notwithstanding shelter provided by the remains of a stone wall which passes over the summit.

Next is a short section of descent south-south-west for about 1,420 yards (1,300m) before turning west for the ascent to **Thornthwaite Crag** (784m/2,569ft),

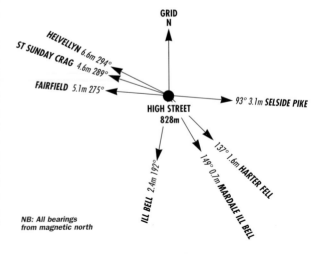

GRID
N

HELVELLYN 6.6m 294°
ST SUNDAY CRAG 4.6m 289°
FAIRFIELD 5.1m 275°

HIGH STREET
828m

93° 3.1m SELSIDE PIKE

ILL BELL 2.4m 192°

137° 1.6m HARTER FELL

149° 0.7m MARDALE ILL BELL

NB: All bearings
from magnetic north

whose summit is marked by a splendid slender cairn over 14ft high. Having left the Roman road, the route now follows a path north-west down steep scree to Threshthwaite Mouth, from where the first real scrambling of the walk is encountered west-south-west up the eastern flank of **Stony Cove Pike** (764m/2,507ft). This appears to be a relatively inconspicuous summit, considering the energy expended in getting there. Here, if visibility is good and the hills are basking in late afternoon sunshine, you will have a good observation point to gaze towards High Raise, High Street, Thornthwaite Crag and Ill Bell.

If you want to take in the summit of **Caudale Moor** (754m/2,474ft), where there is a small cairn, it is only about 550 yards (500m) to the west over easy, slightly undulating terrain. From there a descent is made south-south-west to John Bell's Banner (if Caudale Moor has been excluded, it is about 600 yards (550m) west of Stony Cove Pike).

5 AS you make your way down from Caudale Moor south-westerly towards **Pike How** (632m/2,072ft) you will come upon a memorial to a former proprietor of the Kirkstone Pass Inn, Mark Atkinson, and his son William Ion Atkinson, suitably placed overlooking the inn with Lake Windermere and Morecambe Bay beyond.

You may notice, too, a change in the breed of hill sheep: up to this point most of the hill ewes and lambs have been Swaledales, indigenous to the Yorkshire Dales, but from here there is a predominance of

■ *Kirkstone Pass Inn from Kilnshaw Chimney*

Herdwicks. This breed, which some claim to have originated in Scandinavia and others in Spain, is normally only to be found in the fells of Lakeland. The sheep are hardy, agile, good-natured, and have the odd characteristic of changing colour as they get older. Lambs are born a very dark chocolate brown, almost black, but as they get older their fleece turns lighter brown and then grey.

❻ THE track descends in a south-westerly direction over Pike How, west of the summit cairn, to a mossy depression from which, after a short ascent, you are able to traverse St Raven's Edge, a peculiar name for a fell.

This lies immediately above the Kirkstone Pass Inn, ideally situated for overnight lodging. It is essential to book well in advance: if accommodation is not available here, the nearest alternative is in Troutbeck, a lengthy diversion away.

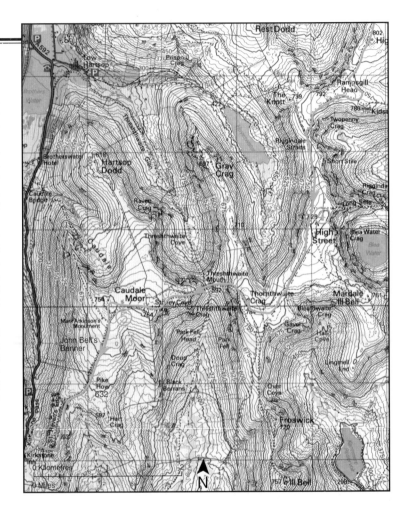

■ *Red Tarn and Striding Edge below Helvellyn*

DAY 3: Kirkstone Pass to Patterdale

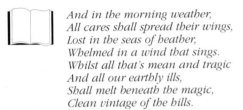

And in the morning weather,
All cares shall spread their wings,
Lost in the seas of heather,
Whelmed in a wind that sings.
Whilst all that's mean and tragic
And all our earthly ills,
Shall melt beneath the magic,
Clean vintage of the hills.

- ❑ **Distance:** 8 miles (12.87 km)
- ❑ **Ascent:** 826m (2,710ft)
- ❑ **Descent:** 1,122m (3,681ft)
- ❑ **Major summits: Red Screes, Dove Crag, Hart Crag, Fairfield, St Sunday Crag**
- ❑ **Going: Stiff climb with some scrambling to top of Red Screes; otherwise moderately strenuous over firm ground on well-defined paths**
- ❑ **Time taken:** 6.5 hours

THE words of this verse by some writer unknown, that I learned from my father on our farm in Cumbria, filled my head as I made may way towards Scandale Pass from my overnight stop at Kirkstone Pass Inn. There, overcast skies had greeted the dawn but it was still dry. Just as I was leaving the inn, a salesman entered, bearing tidings of a change in the weather, and as I made for Kilnshaw Chimney a stiff breeze was blowing.

Looking back down the valley, I was saddened by the sight of quarrying on the eastern face of Snarker Pike which makes a considerable and unsightly scar on the fellside.

I enjoyed a well-earned lunch behind the windbreak on the summit of Fairfield, sparing a thought for a former walking colleague who died a few years ago in a fall on Helvellyn. The fells can be a dangerous place, especially in winter, and, indeed, on the occasion I recalled when we had walked together on Fairfield, we had had to amend our route when one of the party began to suffer from mild hypothermia. Today's weath-er posed no such threat and, later, descending from Cofa Pike, I came upon a large group of elderly walkers who seemed quite undeterred by the steepness of their ascent. I overheard one member of the party wonder how I managed to keep my hat on my head in such a wind. But then she was quite unaware of that marvel of millinery technology, the chin strap.

I arrived at Patterdale Youth Hostel just as the salesman's foreboding turned to actual rain – timing which seemed fortuitous but might, I hoped, have been a

■ *Dollywaggon Pike, Nethermost Pike and Helvellyn from Birks Fell*

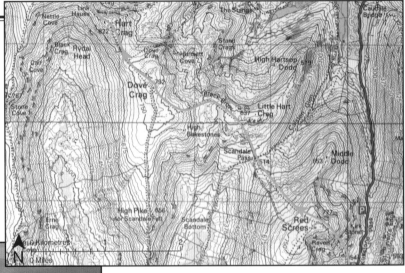

divine blessing. The hostel provides excellent accommodation, and I met a number of people on Wainwright's Coast to Coast Walk.

Among them was one elderly lady from Llandudno who was undertaking the challenge alone. She had a very deep Christian faith, and her face radiated the love of God. I considered it very much a privilege to share fellowship with her.

■ *Brothers Water and*
High Hartsop Dodd from Red Screes

1 FROM the summit of Kirkstone Pass, the route goes north-west on a steep traversing and ascending path up the easterly ridge of Kilnshaw Chimney to the summit of **Red Screes** (777m/ 2,549ft). Here is an excellent vantage point for Patterdale, Brothers Water and the southern end of Ullswater. To the north-west a series of ridges leads to the summits of Dove Crag, Hart Crag and Fairfield.

2 THE descent from Red Screes to the top of Scandale Pass is easy, over springy turf with the terrain interspersed with rock outcrops. Height is gained over an undulating series of ridges which pass close to **Dove Crag** (792m/2,598ft) and continue north-westerly

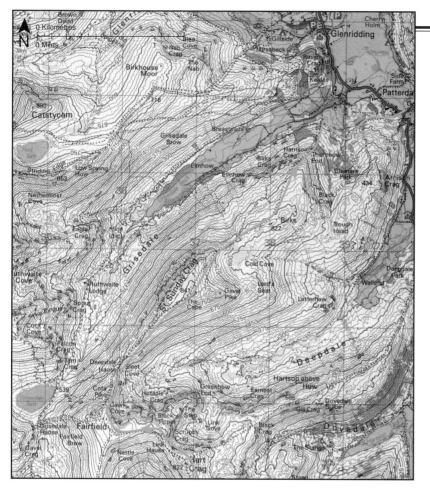

past **Hart Crag** (822m/2698ft) before the final climb west to the flat summit of **Fairfield** (873m/2,863ft), the highest point of the day.

3 HERE is a grand panoramic view: north to Dollywaggon and Nethermost Pikes, with a side view of Striding Edge leading to the summit of Helvellyn beyond. Here, too, is shelter for lunch behind a pile of stones curved into a wind break.

Once a year, in May, runners make their way here on the annual Fairfield Horseshoe Race, covering the summits of Fairfield, Hart Crag and Dove Crag in little more than an hour on a good day. A marshal stands on the top of Fairfield handing out tokens to runners to prove that they have made it; in misty weather he rings a bell to guide them to the top.

The route descends northwards from Fairfield to Cofa Pike: it is steep and requires care, but should present no seri-

ous difficulties to the experienced hill walker. Down to the west you will see Grisedale Tarn. Carry on in a north-easterly direction to Deepdale Hause, from where a gradual and easy ascent leads past a series of false summits to **St Sunday Crag** (841m/2,756ft).

4 HERE, perhaps, is an even more impressive view of Helvellyn and its neighbouring fells. Beyond, to the north-east, lies **Birks** (622m/2,040ft). The descending path provides a splendid vista of Ullswater in all its vary-

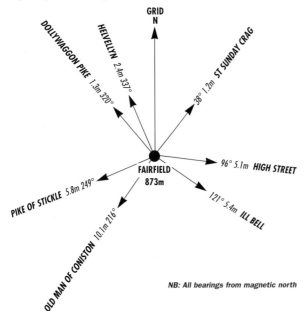

■ *Caudale Moor summit, looking towards Brothers Water and Ullswater*

ing aspects: curving lakeside, tiny islands, and steamers on the boat piers at Glenridding.

5 AT the base of Thornhow End a track leads east to Patterdale village and the youth hostel, which provides excellent accommodation. If an overnight stay has been arranged in Glenridding, from the base of Thornhow End one descends to the road from Grisedale, which meets the A592 road midway between Glenridding and Patterdale.

DAY 4: Patterdale to Threlkeld

THE day started grey and murky, but as the morning progressed patches of blue sky appeared, giving me hope that the weather would hold for my passage over Helvellyn via Striding Edge.

The rain during the night had refreshed the pastures, settled the dust, and cleared some of the haze. As I trudged up the Tarmac road to Elmhow, the soles of my feet felt considerably more comfortable than yesterday, when I had ended up having to soothe them with a soak in cold water. Feet are the walker's 'wheels' and must be looked after: if they give out, the rest of the body soon follows!

The sun was shining now, and with a cool breeze on my face, I felt I was making good going. I kept as close as possible to the crest of Striding Edge. This required some care as, with my large rucksack acting as a sail, the gusty wind tended to disturb my balance. I reached the summit at 11.30 and, moving on towards Swirral Edge, paused a while to reflect on the memory of another old climbing colleague who died here in a winter accident. The mountains we love so deeply and yet which can still be so cruel…

On the summit of Raise, I came upon a jovial group of retired Geordies and ate my packed lunch to the echo of their banter. By the time I reached Great Dodd the wind had increased, with strong gusts across the bare and exposed summit. As I gazed over the Eden Valley

- **Distance: 12.5 miles (20.12 km)**
  Alternative 13.75 miles (22.13 km)
- **Ascent: 1,227m (4,026ft)**
- **Descent: 1,227m (4,026ft)**
- **Major summits: Helvellyn, Kepple Cove, Raise, Stybarrow Dodd, Watson's Dodd, Great Dodd, Calfhow Pike, Clough Head**
- **Going: Strenuous, mainly on well-defined paths; scrambling in exposed places requiring care and experience**
- **Time taken: 8.5 hours**

memories came flooding back of my childhood on my parents' farm south of Carlisle, surrounded by all the delights of country life. From there, the fells of both Lakeland and the North Pennines beckoned from either direction: I could see Blencathra on the one hand and Cold Fell on the other and I would yearn for the school holidays when I would often be joined by school chums to do a bit of scrambling or climbing in the Lakes.

Now, as I reached the old coach road connecting Matterdale and St John's in the Vale, the battering of the wind had left me a little jaded. Then, to cap it all, it started to rain. I halted to don my waterproof, and watched a young man on an autocross motor-cycle riding up and down the lower reaches of White Pike to the accursed accompaniment of snarls and shrieks from his machine.

Finally, I booked into my guest house at Threlkeld and adjourned to the Salutation Inn, with its charming low-beamed ceilings, and walls hung with hunting pictures and memora-bilia. Here in 'John Peel country', I enjoyed my meal and drink to the accompaniment of hunt-ing-songs and ballads (albeit only taped), which rang in my ears as I retired for the night.

■ *Striding Edge and Helvellyn from above 'Hole in the Wall'*

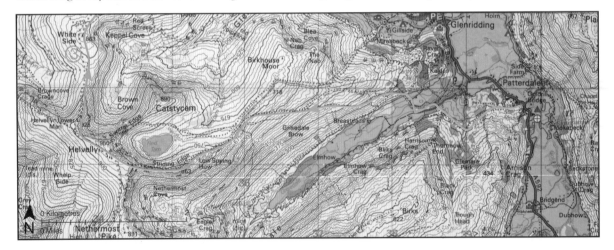

1 IF you have stayed overnight in Patterdale or the Youth Hostel, retrace your steps by the footpath which leads west from the village to the Grisedale road via the bottom of Thornhow End. After crossing Grisedale Beck and making a short direct ascent north-west, a sloping path leads west for about a mile and a half (2.4 km) to a gate in a wall known and shown on the map as the 'Hole in the Wall'.

If you are starting from Glenridding, and want to avoid a certain amount of road walking, you can join the former route east of the 'Hole in the Wall' direct from Glenridding. Leave near the village post office, and take the footpath west on the south side of Glenridding Beck to Rattlebeck Bridge. Climb south-west from here on a path by the side of Mires Beck in Little Cove to join the route from Patterdale.

2 THE 'Hole in the Wall' marks the start of the ascent of Helvellyn following a south-west and then west direction, by the Striding Edge ridge. Higher up, walking the crest of the ridge is a very exhilarating experience, but very great care is required in windy or winter conditions, and as such should only then be attempted by very experienced walkers or climbers, properly equipped. Part-way along the ridge is a memorial plaque to a member of the Dixon family who fell to his death from the ridge in 1858 while fox hunting.

Before the final steep section, which leads to the summit plateau, there is a step in the ridge which requires some scrambling in order to descend it safely

to the neck. The eroded slope of the final section, known as the Abyss, is easier on its left side and should present no serious difficulty except in severe winter conditions, when ice axes and ropes may be required: it should then be attempted only by serious and experienced mountaineers.

At the edge of the plateau at the summit of **Helvellyn** (950m/3,118ft) there is a memorial to Charles Gough, a man from Kendal who fell to his death from Striding Edge while walking with his dog in 1803. It was three months before his body was located, with his faithful dog still standing guard.

The summit of

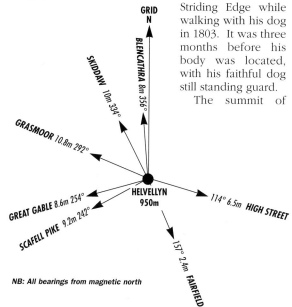

NB: All bearings from magnetic north

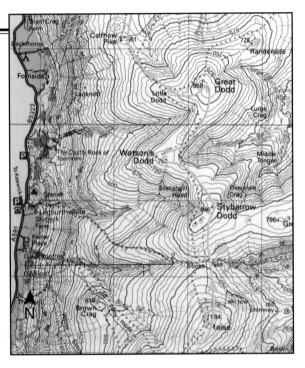

Helvellyn is also famous as the first mountain top in Britain on which an aeroplane landed: Bert Hindle and John Leeming landed an Avro Alpha here on December 22, 1926, and after a short stop flew back to Woodford.

Helvellyn, one of only four mountains in the Lake District over 3,000ft (914m), is immensely popular. On a clear day it provides a magnificent viewpoint from which to observe all the eastern fells and lakes near at hand, as well as those at a greater distance to the west – a scene of unparalleled beauty. It is not surprising that, on a clear day, you seldom have the summit to yourself.

The route now heads north-west for about 765 yards (700m) around the rim of Brown Cove to a cairn on Lower Man, whereupon the path descends north to a cairn at 863m (2,832ft) above Keppel Cove.

❸THERE is a further descent before ascending again north-east to a broad ridge leading to **Raise** (884m/2,900ft), the most northerly fell in the Helvellyn group.

Continue north on an easy descent to Sticks Pass, on the main thoroughfare for walkers between Glenridding and Thirlmere, a pleasant and convenient path linking one valley to another. The fells to the north are **Stybarrow Dodd** (846m/2,776ft), **Watson's Dodd** (789m/2,589ft) and **Great Dodd** (858m/2,815ft), all part of Matterdale Common. These are rolling, grassy hills, and in good visibility give views over the vast Eden Valley to the Scottish Border hills, eastward to the north-

ern end of the Pennines and the Tyne Gap, north-west to the Solway Firth and the Galloway Hills beyond.

❹FROM Sticks Pass, follow the track north, making slight detours to take in the various tops, because for reasons unknown the track bypasses all the Dodd Fells. At the northern end of the group, descend in a north-westerly direction to **Calfhow Pike** (661m/ 2,166ft), a citadel-shaped rocky outcrop.

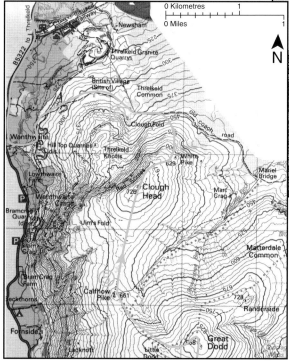

■ *Catstycam and mist-shrouded Keppel Cove*

Threlkeld village over Threlkeld Common. If permission from the land owner, Lowther Estates, is not obtained, then the route to follow is by continuing along the old coach road, north-west and then south-west, to Hill Top Farm, and then taking the B5322 road north to Threlkeld village.

7 THRELKELD was once famous for its Cumbrian wrestlers and now for its fell-runners. According to Edmund Bogg, the name "Threlket or Threlkeld, is said to have come from a Viking name Thorgell, who in the tenth century conquered the Cimbric people and settled in this fair valley"[3]. The village has two inns – the Salutation and the Horse and Farrier – and a number of guesthouses. The resourceful camper will be able to find, with permission, a suitable site for the night.

5 HEAD north up a slight incline to **Clough Head** (726m/2,381ft) which is the most northerly fell of this group. Then go north-east to descend over White Pike to the old coach road connecting Matterdale with St John's in the Vale.

6 THERE is no right of way from the old coach road at Hausewell Brow north-west to Newsham and

[3] *Two Thousand Miles of Wandering in the Border Country, Lakeland and Ribblesdale*, Edmund Bogg, Leeds, & John Sampson, York, 1898.

DAY 5: Threlkeld to Keswick

TRAVELLING from Threlkeld along the old road brought back many happy memories of climbing days with my father, and friends from school and college, and I was in happy mood as I tramped along the road whistling *John Peel.*

My spirits and optimism were dampened somewhat when, as I climbed the hillside above Scales, a young man with small day-pack on his back fairly rocketed past me and disappeared around the corner of the ridge. What it is to have the energy of youth!

Given the wind and prospect of rain, I decided to avoid the potential dangers I might face with my heavy load on Sharp Edge. By the time I reached the summit of Blencathra by the more gentle route, there was indeed a fresh wind blowing from the south-east, and I sheltered to have lunch on the lee side overlooking 'The Back o' Skidda', a vast expanse of open hill country little frequented by tourists. Then it was on towards Skiddaw, resting a moment or two on the bench outside Skiddaw House Youth Hostel to admire the view down the valley of the River Caldew. It was a peaceful, lazy afternoon, and I longed to linger, but I resisted the temptation after reflecting that time was passing all too quickly and I still had some distance to cover before nightfall.

I arrived at the summit and was surprised to find, sitting in the circular stone shelter, the young walker who had sped past me earlier in the day. He turned out to be an Australian from Melbourne. We exchanged stories and

- ❑ **Distance: 14 miles (22.53 km)**
- ❑ **Ascent: 1,352m (4,436ft)**
- ❑ **Descent: 1,412m (4,633ft)**
- ❑ **Major summits: Blencathra, Sale How, Skiddaw, Little Man**
- ❑ **Going: Moderately strenuous over wild open fell with scrambling on Sharp Edge which is very exposed in places requiring great care**
- ❑ **Time taken: 9.5 hours**

I admired the spirit and energy that seemed to epitomise his globetrotting compatriots whom I had encountered on my own journey.

The wind was still blustery as I made my way towards Keswick, but the afternoon was bright with fair amounts of high cloud. I was booked in for two nights at a guest house which, despite being fairly central, proved to be in a relatively quiet area. The summer season had hardly begun, so perhaps it was the lull before the storm!

I was relieved to be at a place of rest, for my feet were somewhat tender. A good hot bath, followed by a delicious meal worked wonders, and I was able to relax after a very pleasant but at times gruelling day's walk.

1 THE former mining village of Threlkeld, situated directly beneath the mountain known as Saddleback or Blencathra, is a good starting point for its ascent, and there are numerous routes by which to do this. One of the most dramatic is by Sharp Edge.

Leave the village by the old road, heading east until it joins the new A66(T) road just west of Doddick. Follow this for three-quarters of a mile (1.2 km) to Scales, where a footpath gives access to the fell behind Scales Farm. Climb the sloping path passing behind and above the White Horse Inn, following the contours around the eastern flank of Scales Fell above Mousthwaite Comb. The route goes north-east, north, and then north-west as it climbs to Scales Tarn.

2 JUST north of the tarn is the start of the ascent to Sharp Edge, one of the narrowest ridges in the Lake District. It is shorter than Striding Edge on Helvellyn, but equally, if not more, testing, and not for the faint-hearted. Great care is required, with some experience of scrambling: a fall from the ridge could be very serious, and it should not be attempted in rain or mist, as the slate becomes very greasy, or in severe winter conditions except by those with winter climbing experience and the proper equipment for snow and ice climbing. After traversing the narrowest part of the ridge there is a section of steep ascent before reaching the broad summit plateau of Blencathra.

A much easier alternative ascent can be made by Scales Fell and ridge, leaving the path to Scales Tarn

above Mousthwaite Cove and heading upwards in a north-westerly direction. This route takes the walker directly to the summit of Blencathra.

From the top of Sharp Edge, going southwards, one encounters a large and then a small cross of white quartzite, memorials to someone, perhaps, or marking the spot where a friend may have died.

The summit of **Blencathra** (868m/2,847ft) is an excellent vantage point for observing St John's in the Vale, Keswick, Derwentwater and the western fells. To the north one overlooks 'The Back o' Skidda', a vast expanse of open fell country formed by Skiddaw Forest, Mungrisdale Common, Uldale, and Caldbeck Fells. It is

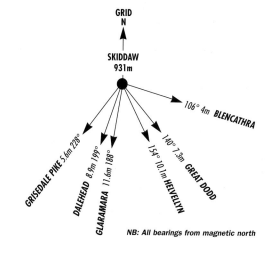

NB: All bearings from magnetic north

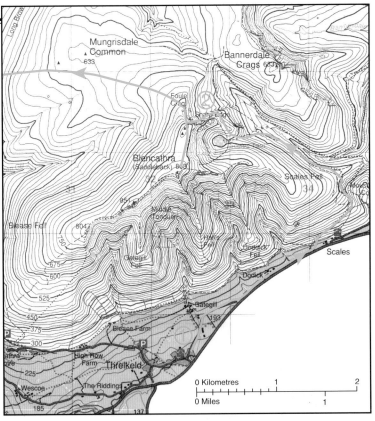

an area less frequented by the Lakeland visitors, and provides a secluded haven for the intrepid rambler who wishes to get away from the hustle and bustle of ordinary life. The Cumbria Way, a medium distance walk of 70 miles (112.5 km) from Ulverston to Carlisle, passes through this part of Lakeland.

From the summit of Blencathra, retrace your steps to the northern end of the fell above Sharp Edge and go north and then north-west to pass **Atkinson Pike** (845m/2,772ft), above Foule Crag.

❸ DESCEND Mungrisedale Common on the broad north-western flank of Blencathra to join the Cumbria Way south of Salehow Beck, a tributary of the River Caldew. Cross this beck by a foot-bridge and head for a remote dwelling called Skiddaw House, a former shepherd's house now used by the Youth Hostels Association. It is in an idyllic situation, relatively sheltered from the westerly winds by a plantation of larch, and offers ideal accommodation for those undertaking the Cumbria Way. Start the ascent of **Skiddaw** (931m/3,054ft) at Skiddaw House, climbing the grassy brow from the northern edge of the larch plantation. Head south-west past a line of grouse butts up to **Sale How** (666m/2,185ft) and on to

join the normal tourist path between **Little Man** (865m/2,837ft) and the final part of the ascent to the summit. This is broad, rounded and exposed to the elements, from which temporary relief may be had in a circular

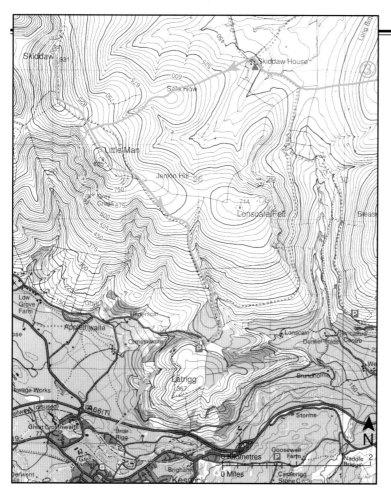

stone shelter. Here are excellent vistas over north-west Cumbria to the Solway Firth and Scottish hills beyond, as well as Keswick, Derwentwater and the central Lakeland fells.

4 THE descent down the much-used tourist path, south and then southeast, is straightforward, though a slight diversion can be made to take in Little Man and Jenkin Hill.

The path to the car park behind Latrigg, past the Hawell Memorial, gives the walker plenty of opportunity on a fine day to gaze on all the different aspects of Derwentwater, Borrowdale and the surrounding fells. From the car park the route follows a section of the Cumbria Way, skirting a plantation and going through woodland at Ewe How to reach the new bridge over the A66 Keswick bypass and the outskirts of the town. Latrigg Fell can be taken in by ascending and descending a path over Mallen Dodd.

5 PASS through Fitz Park and cross the River Greta by a metal footbridge which gives access to the town's back streets and then High Street.

The most prominent feature here is the Moot Hall which, according to

■ *The summit ridge of Blencathra, looking west towards Grisedale Pike and Grasmoor*

Parson and White[4], was formerly the Town Hall, built in 1813 on the site of the old Court House. Materials used for its construction were said to have come from the pleasure house on Lord's Island, on Derwentwater, belonging to the Ratcliffe family.

The bell on which the Moot Hall clock used to strike was removed from the same place and is inscribed '*H.D. 1001 R.O.*'. This inscription is something of a mystery. Experts say the bell was made in 1601, and that the initials stand for Robert Oldfield, a peripatetic bell founder of the early 17th century. The ground floor was once used as a meal, butter, egg, and poultry market, while the upper part was a commodious courtroom where the governors of Greenwich Hospital, as lords of the manor of Castlerigg and Derwent Water, held a Copyhold Court, and also a Court Baron in May and October for the recovery of small debts under 40 shillings.

Keswick has ample facilities: many hotels, guesthouses, a youth hostel and campsites, and also a variety of shops selling outdoor equipment and clothing. The town has very much a holiday atmosphere, and is an ideal place in which to break your journey and relax.

[4] *History, Directory and Gazetteer of Cumberland and Westmorland,* W Parson & W White, 1829; republished by Michael Moon 1976

DAY 6: The Coledale Round

I AWOKE to an overcast day with light rain – you can't be lucky all the time – but I was not too anxious. The going should be easier than on previous days because this was a circular walk and I'd only be carrying a day's clothing and food.

I left Keswick by the old road, a pleasant contrast to the bypass with its noise, clatter and fumes of the traffic, and made my way to Braithwaite, where my entry was celebrated by a plume of dense black smoke rising from a chimney fire.

Up the hill I came across a pair of yellow wagtails, their brilliant colouring brightening what had so far been a dull day. Visibility was poor all morning, and when I reached the summit of Grisedale Pike I saw the ridge ahead of me, westward to Whiteside over Hopegill Head, enveloped in low cloud.

Here I met two girls who had walked up from the Whinlatter Pass on to Grisedale Pike and intended to descend the northern ridge from Hopegill Head on their return journey. I stopped to enjoy my packed lunch and watched them gingerly descending the upper part of the ridge.

Visibility worsened as I headed for the summit of Grasmoor, and as I made my way up over steep rock and grass I thanked those who had established the line of small cairns for lonely individuals like myself rambling over the fells in dense mist. I nearly missed the

- ❑ **Distance:** 18 miles (28.97 km)
- ❑ **Ascent:** 1,594m (5,230ft)
- ❑ **Descent:** 1,594m (5,230ft)
- ❑ **Major summits:** Grisedale Pike, Hopegill Head, Whiteside, Eel Crag (Crag Hill), Grasmoor, Sail, Causey Pike
- ❑ **Going:** Sustained, moderately strenuous, over high undulating ridges on well-defined paths; the alternative is very strenuous with scrambling
- ❑ **Time taken:** 10.5 hours; alternative 14.5 hours

cairn on the summit, which was eerie and bleak, but I did find some company there: a Herdwick ewe and her lamb.

Traversing and contouring down the upper steep section of Causey Pike I fell heavily on wet heather. It was a blessing I had a small rucksack, as otherwise a painful and thoroughly inconvenient injury might have resulted, but even so I found the descent to Braithwaite village wearisome and my pace slow.

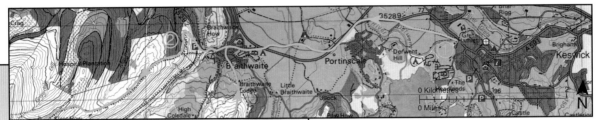

■ **Grisedale Pike, Hopegill Head and Sand Hill from Whiteside**

❶ THIS circular route starts by crossing the River Greta in Keswick and passing through fields to Stormwater Bridge to join the B5289 road east of Derwent Bridge. After crossing the River Derwent, one has to walk a short distance along the verge of the A66(T) road before being able to divert along a section of the former road on the right. This goes past a disused quarry, a war memorial, and over Newlands Beck Bridge before returning to the A66(T), which you cross to enter the village of Braithwaite.

Make your way through the village, along the Lorton/Whinlatter Pass road, and take a newly-restored path of wooden and earth steps near a former quarry. Height is gained quickly at first, but the gradient then eases to the summit of **Kinn** (374m/1,227ft).

❷ FROM here there is a gradual ascent in a south-westerly direction before the gradient increases up Sleet How, over scree, to the summit of **Grisedale Pike** (791m/2,593ft).

❸ AHEAD to the west lies a series of ridges leading to the summits of **Hopegill Head** (770m/2,525ft) and **Whiteside** (719m/2,359ft). The route to these offers pleasant and exhilarating walking, south-west and then west, along the rim of Hobcarton Crag, with its steep cliffs falling away to the north, before ascending to the summit of Hopegill Head. From here the ridge becomes narrower in places as one moves westwards to Whiteside.

4 FROM this summit you have a choice of routes to the top of **Grasmoor** (852m/2,795ft). If you are feeling full of energy and enthusiasm, and there is plenty of time available – beware, this involves an extra

688m/2,257ft of ascent and descent in total – descend the south-west ridge of Whiteside over Whin Ben to the B5289 road at Lanthwaite Green Farm from where an ascent can be made, in an easterly direction, of the west ridge of Grasmoor, which provides excellent scrambling.

The quicker and easier option is to retrace your steps eastward to Hopegill Head, and descend over **Sand Hill** (756m/2,480ft) to cross Coledale Hause. The ascent of Grasmoor is by its north-east ridge, the upper part of

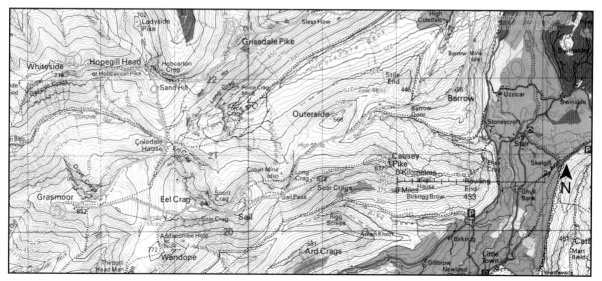

which follows the edge of Dove Crags. These form the south side of Gasgale Gill until the summit plateau is reached.

5 THE panorama from the top of Grasmoor is excellent, and has been described by the late W A Poucher[5] as one of the best in Lakeland. To see the fells resplendent the best time of day to be on the summit is late afternoon or early evening when the sun is sinking in the west, casting long shadows. There are far-reaching vistas in every direction.

To the north lie Whiteside, Hopegill Head and Grisedale Pike. Moving eastwards, there are Skiddaw and Blencathra, the sentinels of northern Lakeland. To the east are the extensive ridges which lead to Helvellyn, with the prominent cone of Catstycam (*Catstye Cam*) on the left.

Moving your eye south-east, the bulk of the central fells come into view, and to the south are the Buttermere Fells of Red Pike, High Stile, High Crag and Haystacks, with Pillar imposing itself above Ennerdale beyond.

On a good day there is a panorama of matchless beauty which is forever imbedded in the memory. There is a gradual descent east from the summit to a grassy col before ascending to **Eel Crag** (840m/2,756ft, and called *Crag Hill* on some maps). There is then a descent over a narrow rocky ridge for a short distance to the summit of **Sail** (771m/2,530ft).

6 AT the col between Sail and **Scar Crags** (672m/2,205ft) there is a choice of routes. You can follow the path over High Moss and along the southern flank of **Outerside** (568m/1,863ft) to Stile End, and then ascend **Barrow** (456m/1,494ft) before descending gently to Braithwaite.

7 FROM here you retrace your steps of the outward journey, by road and path, to Keswick.

The alternative is to continue over Scar Crags from the col to **Causey Pike** (637m/2,090ft) and then descend via **Rowling End** (433m/1,422ft) to the hamlet of Stair. From north-east of Stair a footpath follows the east bank of Newlands Beck to the A66(T), from which Keswick is reached.

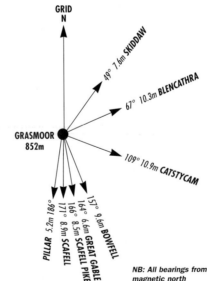

GRID N

49° 7.6m SKIDDAW
67° 10.3m BLENCATHRA
109° 10.9m CATSTYCAM

GRASMOOR 852m

PILLAR 5.2m 186°
171° 8.9m SCAFELL
166° 8.5m SCAFELL PIKE
164° 6.6m GREAT GABLE
157° 9.6m BOWFELL

NB: All bearings from magnetic north

[5] *The Lakeland Peaks*, W A Poucher; Published by Constable & Co; 9th edition 1983

DAY 7: Keswick to Buttermere

A BRIGHT, beautifully clear morning was a delight on what would mark a significant milestone on my journey. The contrast with the previous day's dreary weather put me in philosophical mood, as I breathed in the scent of the sun-drenched azaleas on the outskirts of Keswick and reflected that the appreciation of life's joys would not be the same without the contrast of sorrows and difficulties.

By the time I reached Buttermere Youth Hostel that night I would have achieved about 95 miles, more than half the total of my challenge, and my spirits began to rise accordingly.

The morning's route took me through woodland full of joyful birdsong, and then to the foot of Catbells (*Cat Bells*) where two American military aircraft swept low overhead and sent a buzzard soaring from its morning perch. By 11 o' clock I was on Catbells — in all the years of my connections with the Lake District, this was the first occasion that I had been on this summit. It amazes me how one or two hills have succeeded in eluding me for one reason or another.

At the top of Dalehead (*Dale Head*), enjoying a late lunch, were numerous walkers, some of whom I had last seen in Patterdale. They threw their leftovers to two Swaledale sheep, who have clearly come to realise that walkers and climbers frequently sit beside summit cairns gorging packed lunches and leaving titbits. The scav-

- **Distance: 11 miles (17.70 km)**
- **Ascent: 1,130m (3,707ft)**
- **Descent: 1,070m (3,510ft)**
- **Major summits: Catbells, Maiden Moor, High Spy, Dalehead, Robinson**
- **Going: Mildly strenuous on well-defined paths through woodland, pastures and open fell**
- **Time taken: 7.5 hours**

engers serve a useful purpose clearing up food left by apathetic tourists, but can not do anything about the plastic and tin waste that litters the more popular hills.

On the summit of Robinson I realised with some alarm that it was a whole 25 years since I had last been here — how time flies. I wondered whether the name of the hill was connected with the one-time landlord by that name at the Fish Inn, Buttermere, an important character in Melvyn Bragg's *The Maid of Buttermere*.

The lake was sparkling in the late afternoon sunshine as I traversed down towards Buttermere. The bright red sail of a dinghy emphasised the contrasting blue water and the lush green of the surrounding fields. What a pic-

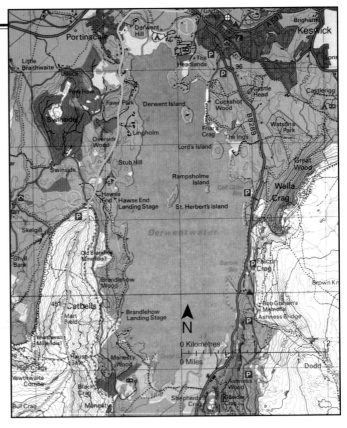

ture! Although my initial anxiety about the journey had now all but disappeared, caution still prevailed, and I was only too well aware of the dangers of being over-confident or complacent. I still had a long way to go, which would require all my energy, care and concentration.

It had been a day of meeting acquaintances from earlier days on my journey, and the day was not to end before I met more. Friends from Northallerton were in the youth hostel, and we adjourned to the Bridge Hotel for a very convivial evening discussing recent exploits.

1 SET off from Keswick, crossing the River Greta at the northern end of the High Street and turning left to walk through fields to the former road leading to the village of Portinscale. The river is followed downstream and crossed by a suspension footbridge which replaced a road bridge swept away in a storm.

Portinscale has a quiet, relaxed atmosphere created by attractively laid-out gardens where rhododendrons, azaleas and poppies provide a rich array of colour in the summer. There are numerous hotels and guest houses which blend unobtrusively into the quaint tranquil environment of the village. Past the post office, head south on the road to Swinside for half a mile (0.8km), where a footpath indicator marks a path through dense deciduous woodland. Walking through this is pure delight, especially in spring and early summer when the leaves display a great variety of shades of green, and the air is full of joyful singing birds. The path passes Lingholm, a large country residence near the shores of Derwentwater, where the gardens, plant centre and tea rooms are open to the public from April to October. The

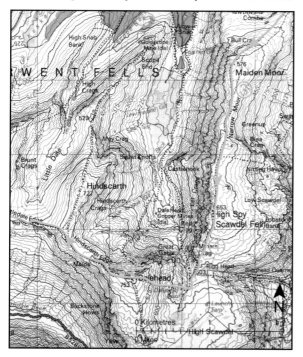

route continues through more mixed woodland and then into a park before it crosses a cattle grid and reaches the road leading to Grange in Borrowdale and the foot of the northern ridge of **Catbells** (451m/1,481ft).

❷ THE path south to the summit is much used and well-marked, and as you gain height there are fine views over Derwentwater to Skiddaw and Blencathra. To the east lie the rolling Dodd Fells leading south to Helvellyn, while to the west are the fells of the previous day's walk: Causey Pike, Eel Crag, Grasmoor and Grisedale Pike. The summit is a good vantage point from which to study the relatively secluded Newlands valley, with its hamlets and farms, beneath a horseshoe of hills: Maiden Moor, High Spy, Dalehead and Hindscarth. Also visible is the road over Newlands Hause to Buttermere. There is a short descent south before the gradual ascent south-west to **Maiden Moor** (576m/1,887ft) above Grange in Borrowdale.

❸ CONTINUE the ascent south over easy terrain to the summit of **High Spy** (653m/2,143ft), where there is a fine cairn perched above Red Crag, a dangerous area a short distance to the west which must be avoided. Care is therefore especially necessary in mist or inclement weather.

❹ COME down southwards by the path east of the upper rim of Miners Crag to Wilson's Bield and Dalehead Tarn. From here you can either climb to **Dalehead** (753m/2,473ft) by the path leading west, which skirts the southern edge of the tarn, or go by the eastern flank of the fell above Great Gable (not to be confused with the mountain of the same name) and

■ *Dalehead from below High Spy summit*

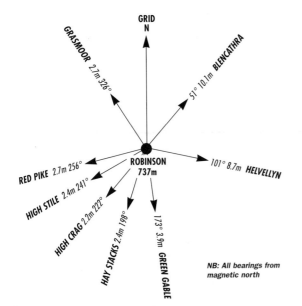

GRID N

GRASMOOR 2.7m 326°

51° 10.1m BLENCATHRA

RED PIKE 2.7m 256°

ROBINSON 737m

101° 8.7m HELVELLYN

HIGH STILE 2.4m 241°

HIGH CRAG 2.2m 222°

HAY STACKS 2.4m 198°

173° 3.9m GREEN GABLE

NB: All bearings from magnetic north

Dalehead Crags, which form the head of the Newlands valley. If you decide on the latter route, there is what seems to be an unending upward struggle before you reach the summit.

5 DALEHEAD offers a splendid vista of the valley below, with the rising slopes of Skiddaw in the background. The summit marks the halfway point of the Newlands Round Walk, and is also significant as the approximate halfway mark on our whole journey along the Lakeland ridges. Descend in a north-westerly direction, on Hindscarth Edge, to a small col and the remains of an iron post and wire fence which can be followed over easy ground along Littledale Edge to **Robinson** (737m/2,417ft), high above Buttermere.

6 THE name Robinson seems synonymous with Buttermere, since the proprietor of the Fish Inn in the early nineteenth century had the same name. His beautiful daughter, nicknamed 'The Beauty of Buttermere', became a legend and featured in Melvyn Bragg's book *The Maid of Buttermere*. From the summit your gaze passes over the dark waters of the lake to the forbidding crags which surround Birkness Comb (*Burtness Comb*) between High Stile and High Crag. Farther east is the ragged outline of Haystacks, with the rounded shape of Brandreth beyond, while north-west lies Grasmoor and its surrounding fells.

The way down is to the west across Buttermere Moss, which even in the summer can be very wet ground. Keep the crags of High Snockrigg on your left, and make your way down over easy ground to a good track leading to a road and Buttermere village.

■ *Maiden Moor from Dalehead*

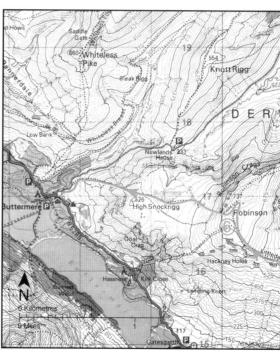

DAY 8: Buttermere to Honister Hause

I HAD less than 11 miles to cover today, but faced the greatest ascent of the journey so far – 1,661m (5,449ft), more than a mile – so I was away from Buttermere Youth Hostel as soon as breakfast and the usual light hostel chores were completed.

The sky was clear, but by the time I had toiled to the summit of Red Pike and reached High Stile, at 11.20, it was quite breezy and a haze had developed. However, the mountains were clear and I made good time to Black Sail Hut, one of the least accessible youth hostels anywhere in England and Wales. Brian Wilkinson was its popular warden for many years until his untimely death (through natural causes) while on holiday in Santiago, Chile, in 1987. He is sorely missed by many who enjoyed his companionship and care at this delightfully remote hostel. The hostel now has a new warden, who welcomed me with a cup of tea, which was much appreciated.

Other walkers and hostellers were gathered around the hostel, including two fell runners who told me about their particular event, in which one runner takes the part of a fox or hare, and the others, who have to find him, the hounds. The pair were brothers, one a diabetic. He was testing a blood sample for sugar levels, and I admired his determination to succeed in the face of adversity.

Later, on the rim of the Westmorland Crags, memories flooded back of the days of my own youth when I

❑ **Distance: 10.5 miles (16.9 km)**
❑ **Ascent: 1,661m (5,449ft)**
❑ **Descent: 1,451m (4,760ft)**
❑ **Major summits: Red Pike, High Stile, High Crag, Kirk Fell, Great Gable, Green Gable, Brandreth, Grey Knotts**
❑ **Going: Very strenuous, with much ascent and descent over mainly broad ridges; scrambling on Kirk Fell and Great Gable**
❑ **Time taken: 8.5 hours**

used to rattle down the screes of Great Hell Gate, determined to do another climb on the Napes Ridges and associated buttresses before it was too late in the day.

Not everyone I met was so full of enthusiasm. Below Windy Gap a young man was urging on his girlfriend who was sitting swearing in total frustration at the prospect of yet more uphill work ahead.

Later, descending from Green Gable, I met a young woman with her son, young daughter and dog. She asked about the time and if she was on the right route for Great Gable. It was nearly 5pm, late in the day to be considering such an objective, and I suggested an alternative route back to the spot where she had arranged to meet her husband. It amazes me how people will venture out on the hills late in the day, ill-equipped, presumably tempted by good weather which can change so easily. It is a wonder that there are not more casualties and people lost on the fells.

By the time I reached the summit of Honister Pass, with its extensive reminders of the old quarrying industry, I was feeling the effects of the day's mile and more of ascent, and a shower, a meal and youth hostel bed were very welcome.

 1 FROM Buttermere village take the lane past the Bridge and Fish hotels and head south across the valley bottom between Buttermere Lake and Crummock Water to Burtness Wood, now in the care of the National Trust. After crossing a footbridge over the outlet of Buttermere, take a restored boulder-laid sloping path, and go south-east through the wood and then south-west up the steep fellside to Bleaberry Tarn. This is a delightful place for quiet reflection while recouping energy for the final thrust to the summit of **Red Pike** (755m/2,479ft).

The route is to the right of the tarn, between Ling Comb and Chapel Crags, up a scree slope that used to be tiring and frustrating – two steps up and one

step down! – but recent path restoration work has alleviated this somewhat. This fell is often referred to as the Red Pike of Buttermere to avoid confusion with another Lakeland fell of the same name.

2 THE summit is a superb vantage point for the four lakes of Loweswater, Crummock Water, Buttermere and Ennerdale Water, plus a wide range of neighbouring fells to the north, east and south – a never-ending panorama of great depth and beauty. Follow a broad, slightly undulating ridge south-eastwards to **High Stile** (806m/2,643ft). A short descent to a cairn at the top of the northern spur of the fell gives a spectacular vista of Buttermere lake with Honister Pass beyond.

3 FROM High Stile the remains of a dilapidated boundary fence lead you south-east to **High Crag** (744m/2,443ft), from where Gamlin End is descended by a steepish scree slope, much eroded in places, to **Seat** (561m/1,840ft).

■ *Buttermere and Crummock Water from Brandreth*

■ Grasmoor, Whiteless Pike, Eel Crag, Sail and Causey Pike from High Stile

4 ANOTHER short steep descent east takes you to the top of Scarth Gap Pass, the main pedestrian thoroughfare between the Buttermere Valley and Ennerdale. Beyond to the east is the rugged fell of Haystacks with its inconspicuous tarns and rocky outcrops, another favourite haunt of the late Alfred Wainwright.

Go south, following the path beside Scarth Beck for about 380 yards (350m) and then bear south-east to take the path that leads along the northern side of a coniferous plantation to Black Sail Hut, the remotest youth hostel in Lakeland and a convenient and often entertaining spot for a midday break to renew energy that will be required for the rest of the day's objectives.

5 FROM the hostel, follow the bottom of the Ennerdale Valley south-east until the path crosses the River Liza just before its confluence with Sail Beck. Turn south here, along the west side of Sail Beck, and stay on the path where it leaves the beck after about

750 yards (700m) from the River Liza and heads south-west up to the summit of Black Sail Pass. This is an important location between Mosedale and Ennerdale and for the ascent of **Pillar** (892m/2,927ft) to the north-west and **Kirk Fell** (802m/2,631ft) to the south-east.

6 FROM the top of the Pass, go south up the steep northern rocky spur of Kirk Fell. Some sections require care, as scrambling is involved, but it should all be within the easy grasp of an experienced fell walker. You emerge on the broad north-west shoulder of

■ Below: Great Hell Gate from Great Gable

the somewhat hump-like fell, with the summit appearing deceptively near. A line of old metal fence posts leads to the top – worth remembering if you are on the mountain in mist, as happened to the writer some years ago when, in dense mist, the fence was not followed: the result was a tricky descent down steep scree to Mosedale. Kirk Fell summit is relatively uninspiring, but there are interesting and worthwhile views of Great

Gable and the Napes Ridges, together with those of Lingmell, Scafell Pike and Scafell.

From the summit, descend past Kirkfell Tarn, initially north-east on a broad ridge and then east over easy ground before the ridge narrows and steepens over Rib End to Beck Head, which can be a confusing place in dense mist. From here there is a steep and sustained

GRID
N

GRASMOOR 6.6m 344°

HIGH STILE 3.7m 321°

18° 12.1m SKIDDAW

PILLAR 2.6m 297°

56° 10.3m GREAT DODD

74° 8.5m HELVELLYN

GREAT GABLE
899m

119° 4.3m PIKE OF STICKLE

176° 2.0m SCAFELL PIKE

NB: All bearings from magnetic north

climb by a well-marked path, first east and then south-east, to **Great Gable** (899m/2,949ft).

7 THIS is one of the more conspicuous and better known summits in Lakeland. Great Gable is the centre of a large area of the Lakeland Fells acquired by the Fell and Rock Climbing Club of the English Lake District as a memorial to members who lost their lives in the Great War. It was later given to the National Trust. There is a memorial here to those who died, and a service is held each year on Remembrance Sunday. Wast Water (*Wastwater*) is a fine focal point from the summit, and the patchwork of small fields around Wasdale Head is fascinating. A short descent south-west to the cairn above the Westmorland Crags is worthwhile for its vantage point from which to view the screes of Great Hell Gate as well as the top of the Napes Ridges.

From the summit, follow the path, eroded and steep in places but well-marked with cairns, north-east to Windy Gap. There is then a short and easy climb to **Green Gable** (801m/2,628ft). From the summit the route goes north on easy terrain along Gillercombe Head to **Brandreth** (715m/2,344ft).

8 CONTINUE north-east to **Grey Knotts** (697m/ 2,287ft). These last three summits are situated above crags which offer a variety of rock climbs for those so inclined and experienced.

9 THERE is a relatively easy descent north-east to Honister Hause. Accommodation is available here at the youth hostel – advance booking is advisable – or further down in the Borrowdale valley.

DAY 9: Honister Hause to Wasdale

IT was a bright but cloudy morning as I descended from the top of Honister to Seatoller by the old road, recalling the last time I had come this way, in September 1985, when undertaking the Coast to Coast Walk for a local church restoration appeal.

It was a day for memories. Passing through the village of Seatoller brought back the day in 1972 when I stopped at the Yew Tree Restaurant and enjoyed the largest breakfast of ham, bacon and eggs it has ever been my good fortune to experience.

On Thorneythwaite Fell two climbers passed me, heading quickly upwards for Raven Crag, and as I looked up towards Comb Door I recalled happy days rock climbing in the area. I also remembered the last time I had been on this particular fell, on a glorious day in May 1983, when undertaking a circuitous walk from Langdale with my faithful labrador, Teal. I recalled resorting to pushing Teal up a narrow gully on our ascent of Glaramara and memories of him were revived again as I descended to the small tarn in which he loved to bathe.

I was saddened as I joined the 'motorway' of a tourist route to Scafell Pike to see how the path had deteriorated and broadened, and I recalled how much narrower and less conspicuous it was in the early Fifties. As I trudged up the back of Great End I noticed a patch of snow and was unable to resist the temptation to leave the path and traverse up it. It was good to feel and hear

- ❑ **Distance:** 11 miles (17.7 km)
- ❑ **Ascent:** 1,262m (4,140ft)
- ❑ **Descent:** 1,542m (5,059ft)
- ❑ **Major summits:** Glaramara, Allen Crags, Great End, Broad Crag, Scafell Pike, Lingmell
- ❑ **Going:** Moderately strenuous over broad ridges; short section of scrambling near Glaramara summit
- ❑ **Time taken:** 8 hours

the crunch of snow beneath my feet, bringing back happy memories of winter climbing days in Scotland.

Visibility was quite good all day, and — having reached the summit of England's highest mountain at 2.30 — the afternoon sun cast shadows over the western slope of Great Gable to create the classic picture seen so often in books. Halfway to Lingmell Crag I waited nearly an hour for the sun to strike Great Gable so that I could take the photograph I wanted, but in vain.

My bed for the night in Wasdale was at Burnthwaite, a Lakeland farmhouse tenanted from the National Trust and offering a warm welcome, good accommodation and excellent food.

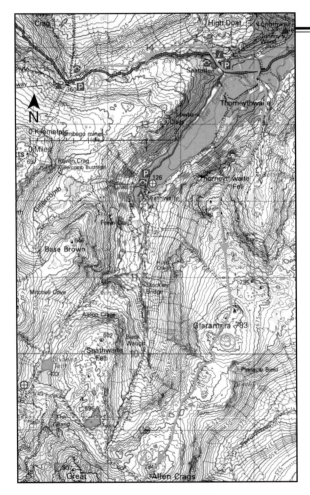

❶ FROM Honister Hause the day begins with a descent to Seatoller, by the old road which now forms part of the popular Coast to Coast Walk from St Bees in Cumbria to Robin Hoods Bay in North Yorkshire. The upper Borrowdale valley is attractively visible, with Thorneythwaite Fell and Glaramara above. Passing through Seatoller village, follow the Borrowdale road towards Rosthwaite until you cross Strands Bridge. Turn immediately right onto a side road leading to Thorneythwaite Farm and, after a bend in the river, cross a stile on the left into a field. A track leads across the field and into woodland which brings you out on the north-east ridge of Thorneythwaite Fell.

❷ THE ascent gives views south-west over the upper Borrowdale valley and south-east across the Combe to Dovenest Crag, once the haunt of rock climbers but now carrying warning notices about rock instability following an earth tremor in December 1978. Follow the path up the fell south-west veering south. It is relatively steep in sections but eases off before a final scramble up a shallow rocky gully takes you to the summit of **Glaramara** (783m/ 2,569ft). From here there is a truly magnificent and memorable vista north down Borrowdale over Rosthwaite Fell and King's How to Derwentwater, with Skiddaw prominently visible beyond.

❸ THE ridge south-west is broad and undulating, interspersed with rocky outcrops and the odd small tarn, and leading over easy terrain to **Allen Crags** (784m/2,572ft).

❹ THE summit is a watershed between the upper regions of Borrowdale, Langstrath and Langdale valleys. Great Gable can be seen to the north-west, with

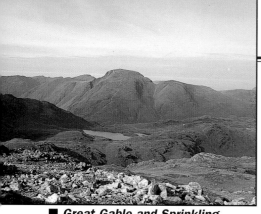

■ *Great Gable and Sprinkling Tarn from Allen Crags*

Sprinkling Tarn in the foreground, and Great End, with its South-East, Central and Cust's gullies clearly visible on a fine day.

The descent south-west to the stone wind shelter is short and poses no difficulty except perhaps in dense mist or severe winter conditions. Here you join the tourist path heading south-west to Esk Hause and then west to Broad Crag and Scafell Pike, but turn off north-west after you have gone about 630 yards (575m) from the shelter and head north-west to the top of **Great End** (907m/2,976ft). It is worth going to the edge of the crags on their north side, particularly to the top of Central Gully – a popular winter route for climbers – to look down on Sprinkling Tarn and take in the excel-

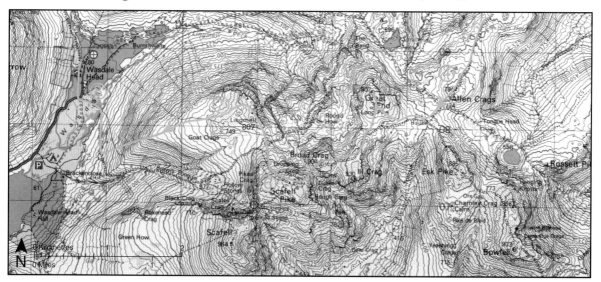

lent views north-west to Great Gable and Kirk Fell as well as north to the fells above Borrowdale.

5 TAKE the path south from Great End over Long Pike to join the normal tourist path towards Scafell Pike. Follow it south-west to Broad Crag, after which there is a short descent to a col and then a short steepish climb to **Scafell Pike** (977m/3,205ft), the highest point reached on the ridge walk. The large summit cairn, once elegantly rounded and tall, has been restored after gradually deteriorating under walkers' feet over the years. The views are superb and far-reaching – Irish Sea to the west, Scottish hills to the north, Pennines to the east and Yorkshire Dales to the south.

6 THE descent is north-west, by a twisting path which forms part of the corridor route to Lingmell Col, from where there is a straightforward climb north-west to the top of **Lingmell** (807m/2,649ft). Walking near the rim of Lingmell Crag provides a splendid viewpoint for Great Gable and the Napes Ridges.

7 A LONG grassy ridge to the west offers the best way down to a permitted path which traverses the western flank of the fell to a footbridge over Lingmell Beck. The path continues through scrub woodland and fields to Wasdale Head.

8 HERE a walled lane leads to the church, situated in a field surrounded by yew trees. St Olaf's is one of the smallest churches in the country, just 40ft by 17ft and only six feet high at one side. Inside is an etching and inscription in a panel of the south window depicting Napes Needle with part of Psalm 121: "*I will lift up mine eyes unto the hills: from whence cometh my strength.*" In the church-yard are graves and memorials to local people and eminent mountaineers, some of whom perished in climbing accidents.

Wasdale Head can be relied upon to provide overnight accommodation, except in busy holiday periods, but there is ample provision for camping.

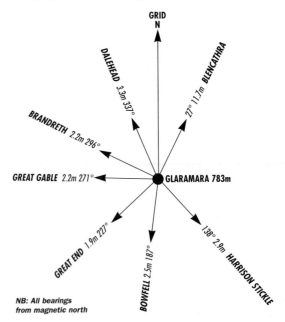

NB: All bearings from magnetic north

DAY 10: The Mosedale Horseshoe

AN overcast morning with the hills shrouded in cloud greeted me as I headed up Mosedale for Black Sail Pass, and much of the day was spent in poor visibility. Looking up to the northern end of Yewbarrow, I could see the prominent pinnacle known as The Stirrup, an awesome sight against the mist.

The last time I had been in this valley was in 1986, around the time of the centenary of the first ascent of Napes Needle by W Haskett-Smith. My labrador Teal and I took the Climbers' Traverse on Great Gable from Sty Head, passing Napes Needle and along to Beck Head, from where we climbed Kirk Fell in very misty conditions. A momentary lapse in concentration took us precipitously down steep scree to Mosedale, instead of the normal route down the steep north ridge of the fell to the top of Black Sail Pass.

A ring-ousel chattered in the bracken to my right, while, above, a skylark continued his serenade. For a while I thought the light seemed to be brightening, but as I crossed the summit of Black Sail Pass just after 11 the mist came swirling impressively upward from the Ennerdale Valley and enveloped me. I ate lunch at the summit of Pillar in a white shroud from which two Herdwick ewes emerged to pester me for leftovers as their Swaledale cousins had on a previous summit.

Had conditions been better, I would have made a brief detour to Steeple, poised over precipitous crags and offering spectacular views, but instead I made my way straight to Haycock and then doubled back over Scoat Fell to Red

> - **Distance:** 12.5 miles (20.12 km)
> - **Ascent:** 1,421m (4,662ft)
> - **Descent:** 1,421m (4,662ft)
> - **Major summits:** Looking Stead, Pillar, Scoat Fell, Haycock, Red Pike, Yewbarrow
> - **Going:** Strenuous over broad and narrow ridges on mainly well-defined paths; scrambling on north and south shoulders of Yewbarrow
> - **Time taken:** 9 hours

Pike, still surrounded by mist and relying on compass bearings to find my way. Stirrup Crag looked forbidding, but it was no time for second thoughts and the ascent provided delightful scrambling, the best of my journey so far.

As I made my way along the northern shore of Wast Water, the cloud rose and the sun broke through at last. It brought out a host of birds: dippers, black-headed gulls protesting as I passed close to their nests of twigs on boulders in shallow water, willow-warblers singing in the rowan trees, and a pair of goosanders diving for food. The walk back up the valley, with Great Gable and Kirk Fell in the background — all illuminated by the late afternoon sun — was a scene to delight any walker.

■ *Great Gable from near Wasdale Head*

1 THE Mosedale Horseshoe is one of the classic walks from Wasdale Head. Set off north out of the hamlet past Row Head. Then go north-west up the eastern bank of the Mosedale Beck, past Ritson's Force waterfall, and follow the path north-eastwards as it climbs to Black Sail Pass.

2 AT the top of the pass take the left-hand path north-west to the top of **Looking Stead** (627m/2,058ft). Ignore the path to the right about 270 yards (250m) west of the summit, which is the interesting high-level route to Robinson's Cairn, Pillar Cove and below Pillar Rock. Instead, carry on west-north-west to **Pillar** (892m/2,927ft), where you will find an Ordnance Survey triangulation pillar and a small stone wind shelter on a flattish summit.

3 HEAD down south-westwards on a broad ridge which narrows as you descend to Wind Gap. There are crags to the north and south and it is neces-

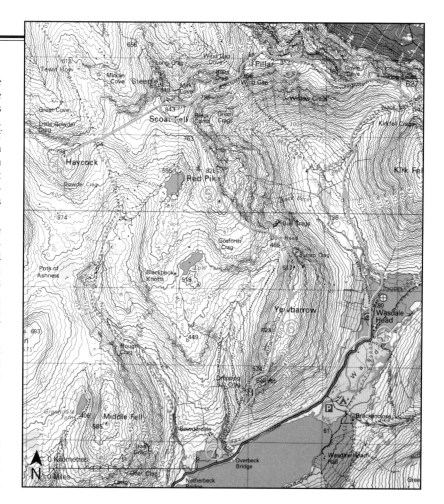

sary to keep to the crest of the ridge. Wind Gap is a high-level and somewhat eerie pedestrian thoroughfare between Mosedale and Ennerdale.

Climb up and follow the track south-west over **Scoat Fell** (841m/2,760ft). Here a stone wall passes over the summit and a small cairn on the wall marks the highest point. On a clear day it is worth making a diversion north to **Steeple** (819m/2,687ft), poised over precipitous crags above Ennerdale. This gives splendid views

of the valley over the shoulder of Black Crag and White Pike towards Pillar Rock, a long-time favourite haunt of rock climbers which attracted such early adventurers as Dr Collie, O G Jones and the Abraham Brothers of Keswick. Its northerly aspect gives it a sombre and awesome appearance when climbing to its base from the forested Ennerdale Valley.

From the summit of Scoat Fell there is an easy route west-south-west across sloping grass to **Haycock** (798m/2,619ft), excluding Seatallan the most westerly summit of the walk.

4 On the summit of Haycock there is a choice of routes by which to return to Wasdale Head. The first alternative is to descend south by Gowder Crag over High Pikehow and Pots of Ashness to ascend **Seatallan** (693m/2,274ft) by its north ridge. Come down from its summit south-south-east to Greendale Tarn and then take the path in a southerly direction to Greendale. From here there is a walk of about 3.5 miles (5.6km) along the road north-east by the side of the northern shore of Wast Water to Wasdale Head.

The better alternative route is via Red Pike and Yewbarrow, which involves some scrambling and offers impressive views over Wast Water, Scafell, Scafell Pike, Lingmell, Great Gable and Kirk Fell. Return to the top of Scoat Fell, take the cairned path south-eastwards over easy ground, and then follow the rim of the crags above Black Comb to **Red Pike** (828m/2,717ft). Near this summit is a rocky outcrop known as The Chair, which has a 'back-rest' of stone with added rocky 'arms'. There is

GRID
N

28° 1m PILLAR

HAYCOCK 1.3m 277°

RED PIKE
828m

97° 1.9m KIRK FELL

115° 4.1m GREAT END

129° 3.8m SCAFELL PIKE

140° 3.7m SCAFELL

SEATALLAN 2.1m 234°

163° 1.4m YEWBARROW

NB: All bearings from magnetic north

■ *Pillar from Red Pike*

known as the Great Door, an opening with vertical walls which provides an excellent foreground for memorable views over Wast Water to the Scafell Crag. The descent requires care, as one descends a gully with much loose rock and scree before reaching an easy grassy slope which leads to Bowderdale and the road running along the northern side of Wast Water.

7 HEAD north-eastwards up the road. In late afternoon sunshine the sight of Great Gable resplendent ahead is a memorable experience as you make your way back to Wasdale Head.

a good vista here over Mosedale to Sty Head, with Great Gable and Great End towering above on either side.

5 FROM Red Pike there is a gradual descent, first in a southerly direction and then south-easterly, to Dore Head, from where it is possible, if circumstances demand, to make one's way down to Mosedale via Dorehead Screes, much eroded in places.

From Dore Head there is a short but steep climb south-south-east up Stirrup Crag and then a scramble to the ridge leading south to **Yewbarrow** (628m/2,058ft), which has a delightfully airy aspect and a magnificent panorama of the neighbouring fells.

6 THE way down is by a small path to the south-west, passing a rock formation

■ *Wast Water and The Screes from Yewbarrow*

■ *Above: Hollow Stones, Pikes Crag and Scafell Crag from Wasdale*

■ *Right: Scafell Pike and Stirrup Crag from Dore Head*

DAY 11: Wasdale to Eskdale

I SET off in a gentle drizzle and at about 450m (1,500ft) entered dense mist and an eerie silence. At the large boulder which marks the point where you leave the tourist path up Scafell Pike and head for Lord's Rake and the north face of Scafell, I was joined by three sturdy-looking young men from Salford. They intended to climb Scafell, but were unsure which way to go in the mist. I said I was going their way, via Lord's Rake.

This classic traverse is badly eroded these days, slippery in the wet and recommended only for the serious walker or climber, and we ascended gingerly through the mist. On the summit of Scafell the atmosphere was still and eerie, but a growing brightness suggested that the sun might break through. Being 20 minutes ahead of time, I stopped for refreshment and in the hope of taking photographs.

Just before reaching the top of Great How I came upon a small piece of aluminium which I deduced had come either from the remains of one of the many aircraft that came to grief in these mountains during the war, or part of an aircraft lost during flight since that time.

The cloud over the highest mountains continued to rise, and soon the entire Scafell range was clear, unveiling an outstanding panorama. In view of this I diverted my descent to include High Scarth Crag and Silverybield

> ❑ **Distance:** 7.5 miles (12.07 km)
> ❑ **Ascent:** 894m (2,933ft)
> ❑ **Descent:** 894m (2,933ft)
> ❑ **Major summits:** Scafell, Slight Side
> ❑ **Going:** Strenuous with scrambling on Lord's Rake and West Wall Traverse, very exposed and requiring very great care; the alternative route avoids this
> ❑ **Time taken:** 8 hours

Crag, hoping for better photographs, but unfortunately the cloud suddenly descended again on the highest tops, and the chance was lost.

I was booked into a farmhouse in Eskdale for the night because the youth hostel was full, but I made my way to the hostel all the same to renew my acquaintance with the warden and his wife, whom I had previously met at Kirkby Stephen Youth Hostel when I was doing the Coast to Coast Walk. Among fellow travellers at the hostel were members of a cycling club on an extensive tour of the Lake District and northern England. The distances they covered in a single day — more than 100 miles — staggered me and made my own accomplishments sound undeservedly modest.

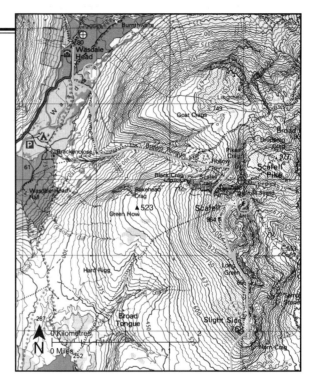

① FROM Wasdale Head retrace your steps of two days ago through fields and scrub woodland to the footbridge over Lingmell Beck. A sloping path leads south then east to Lingmell Gill, from which, after crossing the main beck at its confluence with a tributary, you climb east up the brow of Brown Tongue and into the upland valley, Hollow Stones. A large boulder about 1,100 yards (1 km) from the confluence of becks and crossing point in Lingmell Gill marks the spot where you bear south towards and up steep scree east of Black Crag to the foot of Scafell Crag and the base of Scafell Pinnacle, which is the start of Lord's Rake.

The ascent of Lord's Rake involves scrambling and requires care, as many rocks have become dislodged and the once-attractive narrow gully is now a mud chute. It is recommended only for the serious and experienced walker or climber. Lord's Rake is the only way of gaining access to the gloomy recesses of Deep Ghyll, via the sensational West Wall Traverse, which starts at the top of the first steep section of Lord's Rake and leads to the summit plateau, from where you head south to the top of Scafell. Beware: the West Wall Traverse is not for the faint-hearted, and only those who are fully experienced in mountain walking and scrambling should attempt it, and then only in good weather conditions. Ascent of Lord's Rake and the West Wall Traverse are strongly advised against in wet weather or winter.

To avoid Deep Ghyll, continue along the natural line of Lord's Rake through its two cols and three distinct sections to its southern end, where a path marked by cairns leads to the summit of Scafell.

To avoid Lord's Rake in the ascent of Scafell, take the path south from Wasdale Head towards the campsite and Brackenclose, from where a path continues south through and by woodland to Hollow Gill. From here you head east to a path which in its upper sections meets the southern end of the Lord's Rake traverse.

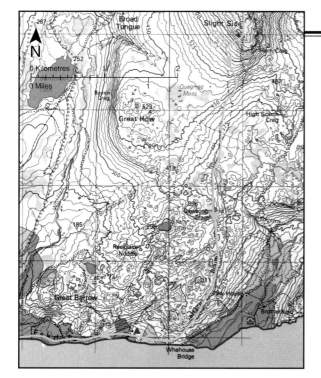

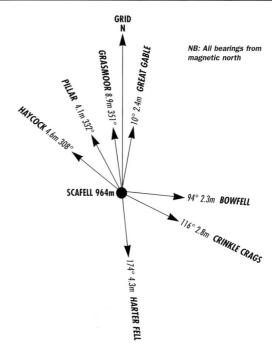

NB: All bearings from magnetic north

GRID N

HAYCOCK 4.6m 308°
PILLAR 4.1m 332°
GRASMOOR 8.9m 351°
GREAT GABLE 10° 2.4m
SCAFELL 964m
BOWFELL 94° 2.3m
CRINKLE CRAGS 116° 2.8m
HARTER FELL 174° 4.3m

❷ THE summit of **Scafell** (964m/3,162ft) is much less prominent than its near neighbour Scafell Pike, and in thick mist it would be easy to miss the summit cairn.

In clear weather the view unfolds south across Eskdale to Harter Fell and its neighbours Hard Knott, Border End and Ulpha Fell, with the Duddon Valley and Morecambe Bay beyond. From the summit take the path south-south-east, following the rim of the crags to the east, over Long Green to **Slight Side** (762m/2,501ft).

❸ AFTER a change to a south-westerly direction for about 275 yards (250m), near Horn Crag you follow the path south to Catcove Beck beneath Cat Crag. Continue on this path south and then south-south-west by the Terrace Route below Dawsonground Crags and Goat Crag to the Eskdale valley road above Wha House Farm.

4 HERE overnight accommodation may be available. Turning right (west) along the road leads you to Eskdale Youth Hostel and the Woolpack Inn, both of which provide excellent lodging.

From Slight Side, there are two possible deviations from the route described above. One includes taking in the top of **Great How** (523m/1,716ft) to the west. Its summit rocky outcrop offers optional short rock-climbing problems of moderate difficulty before you descend south-east to regain the path beneath Cat Crag.

The second detour, on a clear day, gives a more detailed view of the high Lakeland mountains from Scafell to Bowfell (*Bow Fell*). After passing Horn Crag in the descent of Slight Side, head south-east near High Scarth and Silverybield Crags to join the path leading south-south-west from Cam Spout Crag. This takes you down to Eskdale, passing two attractive waterfalls, at Scale Bridge and above, before taking you through the farmstead at Taw House, and past Birdhow, a quaint 'two up and two down' Lakeland cottage set back from the farm road in a field.

After the cottage take the path left through fields beside of the north bank of the River Esk to Wha House Bridge. Here you turn right (west) along the road to the youth hostel and Woolpack Inn.

■ *'Matterhorn' boulder on Grey Friar*

DAY 12: Eskdale to Coniston

BOB Graham was a teetotal non-smoker who ran a guest house in Lake Road, Keswick. To celebrate his 42nd birthday, this former gardener decided, fittingly, to ascend 42 Lakeland peaks. But this was no ordinary ascent: wearing shorts, tennis shoes and a pyjama jacket, Graham set off from the Moot Hall, Keswick, at 1 a.m. on June 13, 1932 and, within 24 hours he had accomplished his goal, running 72 miles and climbing 27,000ft in the process. During the run, he ate bread, butter and lightly boiled eggs, with plenty of fruit and sweets for energy. His pacers carried his boots, but he did not need them.

I recall this story of remarkable human endurance because later this day, on Grey Friar, I would meet one of the hardy members of the Bob Graham Club who remember their mentor by completing the same challenge in under 24 hours. This chap was 'only training', undertaking a circuit from Langdale, over Scafell, down to Eskdale and Wrynose Bottom, and back to Langdale via Grey Friar and Wrynose Fell. Some training run!

Although numerically a shadow of Bob Graham's achievement, this was going to be a tough day for me, and a prelude to an even tougher tomorrow. And, after all, I did have a rucksack to carry, too. I had set out on a bright, clear morning with high cloud. I was in good spirits as I crossed the River Esk and entered a woodland of young oak, with shafts of sunlight breaking through gaps in the tree canopy in a perfect corner of unspoilt Lakeland.

As I toiled up the flank of Harter Fell, sending the first

- **Distance:** 15 miles (24.14 km)
- **Ascent:** 1,672m (5,486ft)
- **Descent:** 1,562m (5,125ft)
- **Major summits:** Harter Fell, Hard Knott, Grey Friar, Old Man of Coniston, Dow Crag, Brown Pike
- **Going:** Strenuous throughout over open fell and undulating ridges; well-defined way from Swirl Band to Coniston
- **Time taken:** 9 hours

grouse of my journey rising in great agitation, I began to find it hard going under a full pack and felt I had not come to terms with the day's challenge. I recovered by the time I reached Border End, overlooking the ancient Roman fort of Hardknott Castle. Just imagine the lot of the lonely centurion billeted up here in the depths of winter so near the very edge of the empire.

Down by the bridge at Cockley Beck I came upon two farmers gathering suckler cows and calves for a supplementary feed of hay. They seemed happy with the trend away from milk into beef production, which had greatly increased the market price for newly-born calves and suckler cows with calves at foot.

The weather was deteriorating, and small dense black clouds were drifting in from the Irish Sea. However, it

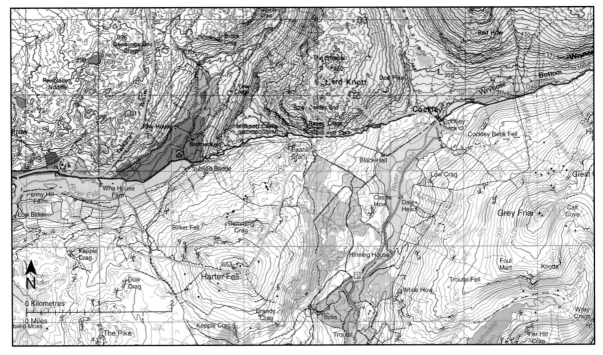

remained dry as I reached The Old Man of Coniston, Brown Pike, and Walna Scar, all of which brought back more memories of Peter, the clairvoyant friend who, as I mentioned earlier, saw the centurion on High Street and died at the early age of 47.

From Walna Scar it was an easy descent to the Coniston Coppermines Youth Hostel, where I arrived nine long, tiring, yet thoroughly enjoyable hours after leaving Eskdale.

❶ THE route from Eskdale to Coniston is slightly longer than those of recent days, and more testing. Start from the Woolpack Inn, and take the farm road south to cross Doctor Bridge over the River Esk and then head east to Penny Hill Farm. Once through the farmstead, take the farm track southwards up the open fell. It joins a wall east for short while and then turns away from it, heading south-east to Spothow Gill. Cross the beck at a con-

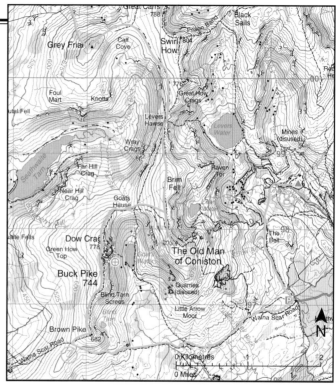

venient point and join a path, marked by small cairns, leading eastwards to the rocky outcrop on the summit of **Harter Fell**, where an Ordnance Survey triangulation point gives a height of 649m (2,129ft), slightly lower than the highest point of 653m (2,143ft).

2 HERE is a splendid vantage from which to gaze down upon the green valleys of the Rivers Duddon and Esk, as well as the broad range of mountains from Crinkle Crags to Scafell.

Descend in a north-easterly direction, along an undulating grass and heather ridge with rocky outcrops, to the top of **Hard Knott Pass** (393m/1,291ft). This, the only throughfare for vehicles between Eskdale, Wrynose Bottom and the Duddon Valleys, is one of the steepest and most intricate mountain passes in Britain, with gradients as steep as 1 in 3 (33 per cent).

3 FROM here it is a straightforward climb, north and then north-west, to the summit of **Border End** (524m/1,719ft), a memorable vantage point for the Eskdale valley and Scafell mountain range. Border End overlooks the ancient Roman fort of Hard Knott Castle (Mediobogdum), with its three enclosed acres, which functioned for a century from about 90 AD.

The route continues north-east to the top of **Hard Knott** (549m/1,803ft) before descending south-east between Slate Knott and Dodd Pike to the Hardknott Pass road. Turn left (east) to the bridge over the River Duddon at Cockley Beck. After crossing the bridge turn right (south) and take the path south-east immediately past the farm and go on through fields to the open fell.

4 THE ascent of **Grey Friar** (772m/2,533ft) is somewhat tedious, south-east and then south via Gaze

Stone How and Copthwaite How, one of the least-frequented fells in Lakeland. The terrain is grass and heather, interspersed with rocky slabs over which it is easier to walk. The climb seems never-ending, but eventually the summit is reached. Here are two small cairns and a curious boulder which resembles the Matterhorn in Switzerland.

5 THE route now goes north-east to the col known as Fairfield between Grey Friar and Great Carrs. From the col take the small traversing path south along the western flank of Swirl How to join the ridge, Swirl Band, which leads south to Levers Hawse, where Levers Water, a reservoir for Coniston, is visible on a clear day to the east. Here you join the well-used broad track from Swirl How to The Old Man of Coniston.

The terrain is easy, the path passing over **Brim Fell** (795m/2,611ft) and round the rim of the cove above Low Water to the summit of **The Old Man** (803m/2,635ft). Here is a large cairn, a few yards south of an Ordnance Survey triangulation pillar made of stone. There are good views on a clear day of Coniston Water, playground for a multitude of sailing craft in the summer, with Windermere beyond.

6 RETRACE your steps north for about 460 yards (425m) and then take a north-west path which gradually descends to **Goat's Hause** (*Hawse*) (649m/2,129ft). From here, with the glittering waters of Goat's Water far below to the south, there is an easy climb, west and then south, to **Dow Crag** (778m/2,555ft), which is poised over precipitous cliffs, the haunt of the

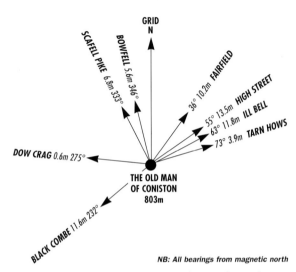

NB: All bearings from magnetic north

intrepid rock climber. In misty conditions, keep the rim of the crags well to your left. Follow the path south along the ridge to **Buck Pike** (744m/2,441ft) and then on to **Brown Pike** (682m/2,237ft) which overlooks the Duddon Valley. Below to the east is the secluded and aptly-named Blind Tarn.

7 DESCEND south-west to the summit of the Walna Scar Road, a much-used pass between the Coniston and Duddon Valleys in the old days when the copper mines and slate quarries were being worked. Follow the Road east and then north-east for some two miles until you reach a gate and a junction with a road leading to the disused slate quarries.

■ *Scafell, Scafell Pike, Broad Crag, Esk Pike and Bowfell from near Spothow Gill on Harter Fell*

8 IF overnight accommodation has been arranged at the Coniston Coppermines Youth Hostel – strongly recommended, as it avoids losing height and reduces the ascent to Wetherlam next morning – follow the quarry road north-west for about three quarters of a mile to Crowberry Haws and then descend the fell-side north to Low Water Beck, where a track leads east to the youth hostel. Alternatively, Coniston village is just under a mile north-east along the tarred road, from the junction of the Walna Scar Road with the road leading to the disused slate quarries.

DAY 13: Coniston to Langdale

THE youth hostel was fully booked, undergoing alterations, and so full of people snoring and sleep-talking that I spent much of the night on the common room sofa, frequently disturbed by the hostel cat. On top of all this breakfast was delayed, and it was 9 a.m. before I got going... hardly a fitting prelude to the longest and most strenuous day of the journey.

The morning started bright, but soon the cloudbase dropped and I made my way up Wetherlam in heavy rain. It had stopped by the time I arrived at Pike of Blisco and decided to have a bite to eat, but the cloud remained low. Parties of walkers appeared out of the mist, exchanged polite greetings, and disappeared again, like ships in the night. It was not until I passed Shelter Crags and started the descent to the Three Tarns that the mist started to rise.

Half way up the scree-lined path to Bowfell I met a walker endowed with a rucksack that looked as heavy as mine. He was wearing a personal stereo and I wondered, not for the first time, why no matter how beautiful the scenery and its attractions of sight and sound, some people still need continual additional noise.

On my way up to Pike of Stickle I passed a little tarn which was another favourite of my labrador Teal. How I wish he could still be with me now. I was saddened by some of the litter lying around and wished people could show more respect for nature.

Coming down from Pavey Ark I halted at the stream to

- **Distance:** 18 miles (28.97 km)
- **Ascent:** 2,131m (6,991ft)
- **Descent** 2,236m (7,336ft)
- **Major summits:** Wetherlam, Swirl How, Pike of Blisco, Crinkle Crags, Bowfell, Pike of Stickle, Harrison Stickle, Pavey Ark
- **Going:** Very strenuous and sustained with much ascent and descent over open fell and undulating ridges; steep in sections with scrambling
- **Time taken: 12 hours**

have a wash and freshen up. I had been going for the last ten and a half hours, and was feeling distinctly tired. The early evening sun was low in the sky, casting long shadows over the hillsides, and it was getting dark as I entered Chapel Stile, where I passed a field of marquees full of the sound of rock music. I made my weary way to the pub known as Wainwrights and ate in a bar crowded with local people and visitors before making my way to my guesthouse.

I had covered more than 18 miles with a combined ascent and descent of 14,000ft. With no snorers or hostel cats to disturb me, I slept like a baby.

CONISTON – SWIRL HOW

1 THE Coniston Coppermines Youth Hostel, at a height of about 195m (640ft), gives a good advantage for the start of what is one of the longest days in distance and has the most ascent – over 2,131m (6,991ft) – of the entire walk. If you have stayed overnight in Coniston village, the youth hostel is reached by taking the untarred road north-west from the village for about a mile and a quarter (2 km).

From the hostel, climb up Coppermines Valley past the old mine workings and head north-west as if heading for Red Dell Head Workings. On entering the upper valley the route to follow is via Moor How, in a north-easterly direction, climbing a grassy slope to join the path which runs west of Furness Fells to Red Gill Head Moss.

From the ridge, follow the path north to the summit of **Wetherlam** (762m/2,502ft) where there is an excellent vantage point for a semi-circular vista to the north from Scafell to Helvellyn.

2 HEAD west-south-west along the path skirting Keld Gill Head to a col at Swirl Hawse from where, by a steep rocky ascent which involves scrambling, you can reach the summit of **Swirl How** (804m/2,637ft), where there is a fine cairn. This ascent, known as the Prison Band, requires care in bad weather, as there are one or two moderately exposed places.

Follow the rim above Broad Slack west for about 165 yards (150m), head north-west for the same dis-

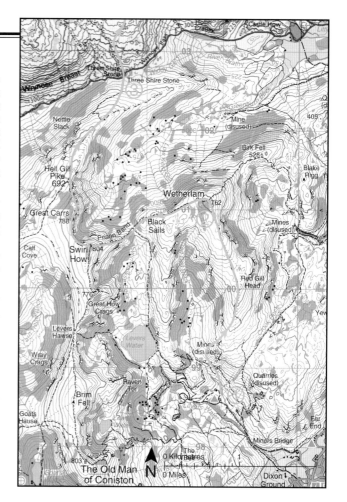

■ *Crinkle Crags and Bowfell from Pike of Blisco*

tance again, and then go north for Great Carrs, Little Carrs and **Hell Gill Pike** (692m/2,270ft). Near these summits there is a large metal cross, surrounded by the debris from a Canadian Air Force Halifax bomber which crashed on these fells during the last war.

From Hell Gill Pike follow the ridge known as Wet Side Edge, heading north-east to the top of Wrynose Pass. Near the summit of this remarkable road is the Three Shire Stone marking the spot where the three former counties of Cumberland, Westmorland and Lancashire converged, and by the strategic placement of legs and arms one can be in all three at the same time. Alas, the county boundary changes of 1974 incorporated Westmorland into Cumberland (renamed Cumbria) and Lancashire, much to the irritation of many Westmerians.

❸ FROM the top of Wrynose Pass take the path leading north-west towards Red Tarn Moss and Red Tarn, but before reaching the Moss, about 700 yards (640m) from the road, leave the path and head north up the open fell to Long Scar, Black Crag and the summit of **Pike of Blisco**

(705m/2,313ft). The cairn on the top was a magnificent sentinel above Great Langdale until 1959, when it became victim to the ravages of man. Today, despite being rebuilt, it is but a meagre semblance of its former self. There are, however, still the fine views down on the head of Great Langdale and the fells which enclose it.

❹ DESCEND south-west, by a well-used and somewhat eroded path to the stream which flows into Brown Gill from Red Tarn. Cross over and climb to encounter a very well-used path between **Great Knott** (696m/2,283ft) and **Cold Pike** (701m/2,300ft). Follow this north-westwards.

If you have time, a diversion to the edge of the crags on Gladstone Knott is worthwhile to see a remarkable rock known as Gladstone's Finger, a slender pinnacle surrounded by a collection of fallen stones. The path leads to the roller-coaster ridge over Crinkle Crags, passing, on the right, steep cliffs with two spectacular gullies before the first top is reached. From here there is an excellent view across Great Cove to the second top with its notorious 'bad step' which is the only awkward section along the ridge. The obstacle, a gully blocked by two enormous chock stones, can be by-passed on the right of the gully up a polished steep wall; the alternatives are scrambling under a huge boulder blocking the scree gully or making a detour up to the left before reaching the gully.

Above the 'bad step' a well-marked track leads to the highest summit, **Long Top** (860m/2,822ft).

5 IN dense mist or severe weather, care and good navigation are required as there are numerous cairns which could lead the unwary walker down into upper Eskdale instead of northwards along the remainder of the Crinkle Crags ridge above Shelter Crags to the Three Tarns.

The traverse of the third, fourth and fifth tops above Shelter Crags is straightforward, followed by a short descent to the Three Tarns, the highest point for walkers traversing the ridge between the Eskdale and Great Langdale valleys. From here, on a clear day, can be seen the Links, a dozen short scree gullies on the south side of Bowfell.

The ascent of **Bowfell** (903m/ 2,960ft) is made by its south-east ridge, keeping clear of the Links on the left. The summit is slightly west of the main track, and easily missed in misty conditions. It is another splendid vantage point from which to gaze upon the majestic Scafell group of mountains to the west as well as across the Langdale valley to Pike of Stickle and Harrison Stickle to the east.

From Bowfell a well-used track marked by small cairns runs north along the north ridge to Ore Gap, south-west of Hanging Knotts above Angle Tarn. Here there is a choice of directions: a rapid descent north to the tarn or, the purist's approach, a climb north-west over **Esk Pike** (885m/2,903ft) followed by a gradual and easy descent to Esk Hause. Turn and head north-east for about 340 yards (310m) to the stone wind shelter, from which a path leads south-east to Angle Tarn, nestling

GRID
N

GLARAMARA 2.6m 325°

ALLEN CRAGS 2.4m 293°

BOWFELL 1.9m 257°

CRINKLE CRAGS 2.2m 230°

PIKE OF STICKLE
709m

113° 4.7m LOUGHRIGG FELL

PIKE OF BLISCO 2.0m 190°

OLD MAN OF CONISTON 5.9m 185°

172° 4.0m WETHERLAM

NB: All bearings from magnetic north

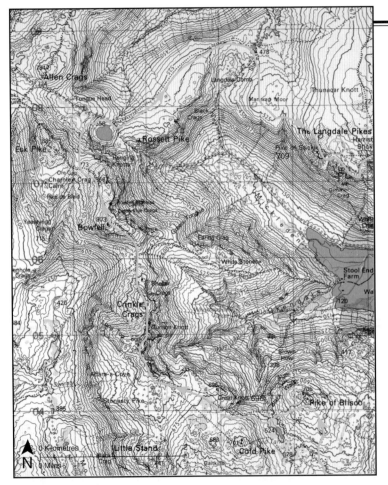

beneath the crags of Esk Pike and Hanging Knotts; only on the brightest of clear days is its gloom dispelled.

6 FROM the tarn follow a small track – missing in its boggiest sections – north-east to traverse the north-west flank of Rossett and Buck Pikes. The path winds round to the south-east and leads eventually to the top of **Stake Pass** (478m/1,568ft), which connects Langstrath and Borrowdale with Great Langdale.

Here an over-used path goes south-east up the north-west flank of **Pike of Stickle** (709m/2,323ft), whose airy summit, poised upon a large rock outcrop, provides a magnificent observation point from which to gaze down on the Great Langdale valley over Loft Crag to Windermere. Some years ago a Neolithic stone axe head was found in scree below the Pike, and further investigation revealed that there had been a stone axe factory there thousands of years ago, exploiting a vein of hard durable stone in the volcanic rocks.

7 RETRACE your steps down the rocky outcrop and then head east for a short distance towards the top of Dungeon Ghyll, from where there is a relatively short, steepish climb to the summit of **Harrison Stickle** (736m/ 2,415ft), the highest of the Langdale Pikes.

The route to **Pavey Ark** (697m/2,288ft) is north-north-east over boulders and rock slabs. This fell has south-east-facing crags providing some good climbs for the rock climber and including Jacks Rake, a narrow inclining terrace which provides a really good airy scramble from Stickle Tarn.

❽FROM the summit of Pavey Ark head carefully northwards for about 100 yards (90m) and find a small, steep, inconspicuous path in a gully leading down the eastern shoulder of the fell, east-north-east, to Bright Beck, which flows into Stickle Tarn. (The alternative is to head from the summit northwest on a well-defined path for about 380 yards (350m) before it turns north-east and then south-east around the north-western shoulder of the fell to the base of its eastern flank at Bright Beck.)

Cross the beck and make a gradual traversing ascent north-east across the southern flank of Blea Rigg and over Great Castle How and Little Castle How. The terrain is undulating and tired legs will feel the strain until the going gets easier towards Swinescar Pike. The route crosses the track from Langdale to Easedale and continues south-east, past a nameless tarn which is the nesting-place of gulls and waterfowl.

Finally you reach Meg Gill, where a path leads down the gill beneath Raven Crag to a road which descends to the village of Chapel Stile.

❾HERE an hotel, public house or guest house will provide accommodation and refreshment for the walker, who will be feeling the effects of a day covering more than 18 miles and more than 4,360m (14,300ft) of combined ascent and descent.

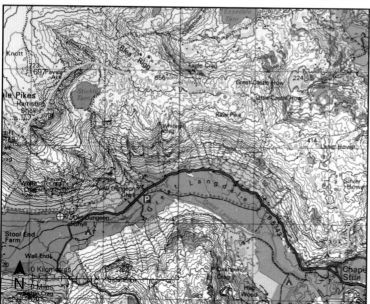

■ *Bowfell from Crinkle Crags*

DAY 14: Langdale to Windermere

IT was a relief to wake up and realise that I had an easy day ahead after two long arduous ones. After a sumptuous breakfast to the strains of Mendelssohn's *Italian Symphony* I set off to climb the hillside above Chapel Stile towards the top of Silver Howe. It was a beautiful morning: bright sunshine, blue sky and scattered white cloud. I felt on top of the world.

Along the ridge to Loughrigg I came across red and white flags placed, it seemed, to mark the course of a fell race. Perhaps they were a feature of the Chapel Stile sports/gala, as fell running has always been a tradition of such events. Its popularity has increased in recent years.

From the summit of Loughrigg, where schoolday memories came surging back of when I first began walking in the Lakeland fells some 35 years ago, I made my way to Todd Crag and the southern end of Loughrigg Fell. Here I was provided with a superb view down the length of Lake Windermere, which was an appropriate and idyllic finish to my walk along the Lakeland ridges.

Descending from Todd Crag I was soon in the hustle and bustle of busy Ambleside, congested with happy holidaymakers. The noise and hectic activity was in complete contrast to the tranquillity of the fells experienced during the last 14 days. I craved more peace and solitude, and, eager to depart the urban environment, I left Waterhead, south of Ambleside, and headed for Skelghyll Wood. It was wonderfully therapeutic to walk through the quiet leafy woodland. I made the short diversion to the top of Jenkin

> ❑ **Distance:** 11 miles (17.7 km)
> ❑ **Ascent:** 773m (2,536ft)
> ❑ **Descent:** 728m (2,388ft)
> ❑ **Major summits:** Loughrigg Fell, Todd Crag, Orrest Head
> ❑ **Going:** Easy over undulating low-level ridges, open fell, woodland and fields on mainly well-defined paths, country lanes and roads
> ❑ **Time taken:** 8 hours

Crag to admire the view across Lake Windermere to the fells above Coniston. Emerging from the woodland, the walk through open countryside to Troutbeck and Orrest Head was invigorating, with all the rich sounds and smells of the countryside in early summer.

On the summit of Orrest Head I paused a while in reflective mood as I gazed with joy and satisfaction towards the glorious fells above Great Langdale and Coniston. I was at the end of my Lakeland Ridges Challenge Walk, but there was a tinge of sadness that it had come to an end. However, all things in life, good, bad or indifferent come to an end sooner or later. This had definitely been one of life's rich interludes and its memory would live on.

■ *The view along Windermere from Loughrigg Fell*

① LEAVE Chapel Stile by the road past the church and retrace the previous day's steps up Meg Gill. At the crest of the ridge go south-east above Spedding Crag, over Dow Bank and towards the top of Red Bank. Lake Windermere becomes increasingly prominent and the hills above Troutbeck – Yoke, Ill Bell, Froswick, all traversed on the first day of the walk – are clearly visible on a clear day.

The terrain is undulating in the descent to the top of

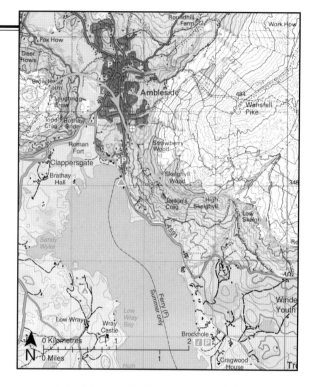

Red Bank, a steep vehicular link between Grasmere and Great Langdale. Cross the road and continue along the ridge, passing through the edge of a splendid stretch of National Trust woodland known as Deer Bolts Wood. Beech, copper beech, ash, oak and sycamore create a canopy for rhododendrons, all of which provide a wonderful array of colour in early summer and autumn.

Emerging from the wood, join a recently restored path, connected to the Loughrigg Terrace path from Rydal Water south-east to the top of **Loughrigg Fell** (335m/1,101ft).

2 THIS is significant, as it is the last summit of any consequence on the ridge walk. Loughrigg Fell overlooks Rydal Water and Grasmere, above which rise the fells of Heron Pike and Seat Sandal. Near Rydal village stands Rydal Hall, now a conference retreat centre for the Diocese of Carlisle; above it, set between ridges leading to the summit of Fairfield, a rhododendron grove makes a vivid splash of pink and red in early summer. To the south, Wansfell quietly overlooks Lake Windermere; to the west Esthwaite Water, Coniston Water, The Old Man of Coniston and Wetherlam come into view. If the day is clear, the panorama is majestic.

From the summit of Loughrigg Fell follow the permitted path carefully in a south-easterly direction through a maze of sheep tracks and minor paths over **Black Mire** (289m/948ft) to **Todd Crag** (212m/695ft) and the viewpoint on the south side of Lily Tarn. Here is a stupendous vista the length of Lake Windermere, an appropriate finale to a Lakeland ridge walk. On the west shore of the lake stands Wray Castle, built for Sir James Dawson, a Liverpool surgeon, between 1840 and 1847 as a Victorian extravaganza. Now owned by the National Trust, it is let as a college and training establishment for marine electronics. To the north of the Castle stands Huyton Hill, a mock Tudor property in the style of Chester architecture which was once an independent school. Below, to the west and east, are Skelwith Church, Brathay Hall Training Centre and the bustling town of Ambleside.

❸ HEAD north-north-east past Lily Tarn to a path leading in the same direction through woodland at Miller Brow before descending east to the River Rothay, where a packhorse bridge leads into Rothay Park and the town.

❹ THE Windermere-to-Windermere circuit can be completed by following the A591 road south-eastwards for about four miles (6.4km), not a very interesting choice and one with the hazard and irritation of heavy traffic during the holiday season. The much more

GRID N

15° 4.1m FAIRFIELD

HARRISON STICKLE 4.2m 293°

65° 6.0m THORNTHWAITE CRAG

79° 5.8m ILL BELL

LOUGHRIGG FELL
335m

SWIRL HOW 5.5m 241°

OLD MAN OF CONISTON 6.5m 229°

135° 5.5m ORREST HEAD

NB: All bearings from magnetic north

attractive alternative is by way of Skelghyll Wood, Town End near Troutbeck, and Orrest Head.

Start from the car park opposite the garden centre in Lake Road, Ambleside, and follow the Old Lake Road for a short distance before turning up a narrow lane near the Glenside Guest House. Climb past Lane Foot and Braeside, and when the lane forks take the road to the right to Jenkin Crag. This leads south-east through Skelghyll Wood and Kelsick Scar, given to the National Trust in 1925 by one Alfred Holden Illingworth in memory of his wife.

From the top of Jenkin Crag a vista of unbelievable beauty unfolds across Lake Windermere to the fells above Skelwith Bridge and, in the background, those above Coniston Water. The path emerges from the woodland just before High Skelghyll Farm, through which one passes before descending the farm road to Hol Beck and a bridleway indicated to Troutbeck. Follow this through open countryside until it joins Hundreds Road.

After this junction follow the walled lane for about 550 yards (500m) and then take a footpath to the right, which descends to Holbeck Lane. Turn left for 110 yards (100m) and then take the bridleway to the right, which descends to cottages. Cross the road and go down a walled lane to two footbridges over Trout Beck. Cross over, and go up a field to the Patterdale-Windermere road.

❺ FROM this point the route is the reverse of that described in the introduction. Walk south towards Windermere for 80 yards (75m) and then take the

■ *Wansfell, Ill Bell and Froswick, with Ambleside below: the view looking back from Loughrigg Fell*

Moorhowe Road to Fusethwaite Yeat. A few yards past the entrance to Low Longmire Farm a footpath on the right leads through fields to Far Orrest and Near Orrest farms. At the latter, skirt the farm steading and when in the farm yard walk past the cottage to take the right fork to the road. Turn right and go west along this road for 270 yards (250m), to where a stile gives access to fields and a path to Orrest Head.

❻ HERE, on a clear day, there may be a last opportunity to savour the magnificent panorama of Lakeland. A stone bench on the summit is inscribed with these lines by Keble:

Thou who has given me eyes to see
And love this sight so fair
Give me a heart to find out thee
And read thee everywhere.

■ *The Fairfield 'horseshoe' from Loughrigg Fell*

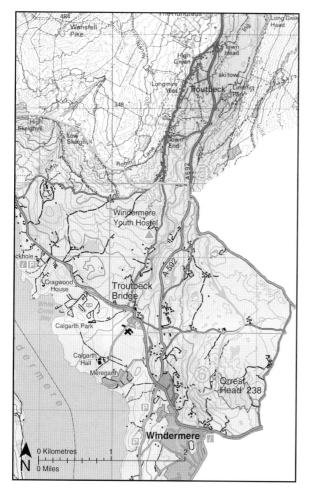

■ *The path to High Skelghyll Farm*
from Skelghyll Wood

Statistics

DISTANCE COVERED:

Total walk, Windermere to Windermere:
180.75 miles (290.9 km)

Total traversing ridges, Troutbeck to Ambleside:
171.25 miles (275.6 km)

Average daily distance during ridge traverses:
12.23 miles (19.68 km)

HEIGHT CLIMBED:

Total walk, Windermere to Windermere:
18,162 metres (59,586 feet)

Average daily ascent during ridge traverses:
1,263 metres (4,144 feet)

Average daily descent during ridge traverses:
1,268 metres (4,160 feet)

DAILY FIGURES:

DAY	ASCENT metres	feet	DESCENT metres	feet	DISTANCE miles	km
Prol.	133	436	137	449	3.5	5.63
1......	1072	3517	948	3110	14.0	22.53
2......	1014	3327	818	2684	14.25	22.93
3......	826	2710	1122	3681	8.0	12.87
4......	1227	4026	1227	4026	12.5	20.12
5......	1352	4436	1412	4633	14.0	22.53
6......	1594	5230	1594	5230	18.0	28.97
7......	1130	3707	1070	3510	11.0	17.70
8......	1661	5449	1451	4760	10.5	16.90
9......	1262	4140	1542	5059	11.0	17.70
10....	1421	4662	1421	4662	12.5	20.12
11....	894	2933	894	2933	7.5	12.07
12....	1672	5486	1562	5125	15.0	24.14
13....	2131	6991	2236	7336	18.0	28.97
14....	773	2536	728	2388	11.0	17.70

Epilogue

NOBODY considering the challenge of the Lakeland Ridges should under-estimate the nature of the task.

The whole 14-day circuit involves more than 18,000m of ascent and descent – some 59,500ft, more than twice the height of Everest – over a distance of more than 180 miles (290km). It is strongly recommended, therefore, that this ridge walk should be undertaken only by physically fit walkers experienced in the British mountains in all types of conditions.

Any time between late April and October might be considered suitable for completion of the walk. The length of daylight in late spring and early summer allows for long days, and the weather, colours and lighting in Lakeland are generally thought to be at their best in April and May. In October, if the weather is good, the autumn colours provide an added attraction for the mountaineer/photographer. During the mid-summer months the weather can be less predictable, and the Lake District is invaded by many visitors who may congest venues and make finding accommodation a problem.

The itinerary suggested in the book envisages walkers staying overnight in hostels, inns or guest houses, and a list of suitable accommodation is given in the Appendix. It may be prudent to book well in advance to be assured of a bed for the night.

There may be Herculean purists who decide to camp throughout the length of the walk. This would require

■ *Great End, from Glaramara*

super fitness to carry the extra weight of camping equipment and food. Careful analysis and planning would be needed to keep the rucksack within a reasonable weight: 14-16kg (30-35lb). On no account should the weight carried exceed one third of the walker's body weight, and anything over 18kg (40lb) would seriously impede progress on some of the more strenuous sections of the walk.

When walking or climbing over the British mountains, especially if doing so alone, it is important to leave behind at your last place of departure a note giving details of the day's route, destination and estimated time of arrival, and to make it known that you have arrived safely.

Above all, heed the advice of the late Edward Whymper and many others: look well to each step, for a momentary lapse of concentration can spoil the happiness of a lifetime.

■ *Bessyboot, Rosthwaite Fell and Raven Crag from above Seatoller*

THE mountaineer Hamish Brown, at the end of his book *Hamish's Mountain Walk*, quotes the Ten Commandments of Mountaineering:

1. Thou shalt prepare thoroughly before starting
2. Thou shalt set out early
3. Thou shalt set out properly equipped
4. Thou shalt choose thy company with care
5. Thou shalt not destroy anything that is thy neighbour's
6. Thou shalt often keep silence to hear the mountain speak
7. Thou shalt leave no sign of thy passing
8. Thou shalt remember others in their strength or weakness
9. Thou shalt bend to the weather and be strong
10. Thou shalt be humble – and praise God.

Little can be added, except to keep your ambitions within the limits of your capability.

Accommodation

A VARIETY of accommodation is available at suitable locations en route, consisting of youth hostels, guest houses, farmhouses, inns and hotels. During the author's traverse six youth hostels, three guest houses, two farmhouses, one inn and one hotel were used.

The youth hostels are strategically situated, and have facilities that cater excellently for the intrepid walker. They also have the advantage of providing a meeting place for like-minded souls with whom to enjoy company and maybe a pint! Overnight bed and breakfast accommodation, with perhaps the provision of an evening meal at guest and farm houses, has a more personal atmosphere, quieter but a little more expensive. Hotels and inns tend to have a more formal atmosphere, catering for the leisurely tourist rather than the active walker.

The standard of accommodation and refreshments during the author's traverse varied from very good to moderate, but in all instances kindness and consideration were shown, and on no occasion was the writer subjected to inconvenience or unpleasantness.

Depending upon the time of year, it may well be wise to book in advance, either one day ahead or for the entire journey before it begins. Advance booking has the advantage of incorporating a certain amount of discipline into the project, with set daily objectives, which is fundamental to a challenge of this nature. From May to October, when the Lake District is extremely popular with holidaymakers, advance booking is strongly recommended.

The alternative, camping, is more flexible – changes of plan caused by bad weather or a decision to abandon the walk will cause few problems – and avoids lost deposits on advance bookings.

Useful addresses:

South Lakeland Leisure Services, Information Centre, Victoria Street, Windermere, Cumbria, LA23 1AD. Tel: 015394 46499

British Rail, Kendal: Tel 01539 720397; Carlisle: Tel 01228 44711; Lancaster: 01524 32333

Lake District Weather Centre, Keswick. Tel: 017687 75757

Cumbria Tourist Board, Ashleigh, Holly Road, Windermere, Cumbria, LA23 2AQ. Tel: 015394 44444

Lake District National Park, Brockhole Visitor Centre, Ecclerigg, Windermere, Cumbria, LA23 1LJ. Tel: 015394 46601

Ambleside Tourist Information Office, The Old Courthouse, Church Street, Ambleside, Cumbria, LA22 0BT. Tel: 015394 32582

Keswick Tourist Information Office, Moot Hall, Main Street, Keswick, Cumbria, CA12 5JR. Tel: 017687 72645

Accommodation suggestions

(Listed in Challenge Walk order are two or three suggestions in villages where accommodation is sparse. Comprehensive lists are available in towns from Tourist Information offices)

Windermere Youth Hostel, High Cross, Bridge Lane, Troutbeck, Windermere, Cumbria, LA23 1LA. Tel: 015394 43543 Fax: 015394 47165

Haweswater Hotel, Bampton, Penrith, Cumbria, CA10 2RP. Tel: 01931 713235

Naddle Farm, Burnbanks, Penrith, Cumbria CA10 2RP. Tel: 01931 713296

Thornthwaite Hall, Bampton, Penrith, Cumbria CA10 2RJ. Tel: 01931 713246

Kirkstone Pass Inn, Ambleside, Cumbria, LA22 9LQ. Tel: 015394 33624

Patterdale Youth Hostel, Goldrill House, Patterdale, Penrith, Cumbria, CA11 0NW. Tel: 017684 82394 Fax: 017684 82034

Saddleback View Guest House, Threlkeld, Keswick, Cumbria, CA12 4SQ. Tel: 017687 79255

Salutation Inn, Threlkeld, Keswick, Cumbria, CA12 4SQ. Tel: 017687 79614

Keswick Youth Hostel, Station Road, Keswick, Cumbria, CA12 5LH. Tel: 017687 72484 Fax: 017687 74129

Glaramara Guest House, 9 Acorn Street, Keswick, Cumbria, CA12 4EA. Tel: 017687 73216

Buttermere Youth Hostel, King George VI Memorial Hostel, Buttermere, Cockermouth, Cumbria, CA13 9XA. Tel: 017687 70245

The Fish Hotel, Buttermere, Cockermouth, Cumbria, CA13 9XA. Tel: 017687 70253

The Bridge Hotel, Buttermere, Cockermouth, Cumbria, CA13 9XA. Tel: 017687 70252

Honister Hause Youth Hostel, Honister Hause, Seatoller, Keswick, Cumbria, CA12 5XN. Tel: 017687 77267

Gillercombe Guest House, Stonethwaite Road End, Rosthwaite, Borrowdale, Keswick, Cumbria, CA12 5XG. Tel: 017687 77602

Burnthwaite Private Hotel, Wasdale Head, Seascale, Cumbria, CA20 1EX. Tel: 019467 26242

Wasdale Head Hotel, Lingmell House, Wasdale Head, Seascale, Cumbria, CA20 9EX. Tel: 019467 26009/26011

Eskdale Youth Hostel, Boot, Holmrook, Cumbria, CA19 1TH. Tel: 019467 23219

Woolpack Inn, Boot, Holmrook, Cumbria, CA13 1TH. Tel: 019467 23230

Wha House Farm, Boot, Holmrook, Cumbria, CA13 1TH. Tel: 019467 23212

Coniston Coppermines Youth Hostel, Coppermines House, Coniston, Cumbria, LA21 8HP. Tel: 015394 41261

Old Dungeon Ghyll Hotel, Great Langdale, Nr Ambleside, Cumbria, LA22 9JY. Tel: 015394 37272

South View Guest House, Chapel Stile, Nr Ambleside, Cumbria, LA22 9JJ. Tel: 015394 37248

Ambleside Youth Hostel, Waterhead, Ambleside, Cumbria, LA22 0EU. Tel: 015394 32304 Fax: 015394 34408

Equipment

ANYONE who has had experience of trekking, long mountain walks or climbing expeditions will understand that an essential part of the planning of any venture is the detailed attention given to the equipment to be carried.

Deciding on the appropriate items to be taken, testing them, and restricting them to the absolute essentials to keep the overall weight to the recommended figure of about 30 lbs (almost 14 kg) is often one of the pre-venture enjoyments. The importance of restricting the overall weight cannot be over-emphasised. Excessive weight requires more physical effort which causes an increase in perspiration, resulting in dehydration, sore feet and unnecessary fatigue which could jeopardise the success of the walk.

A robust, comfortable rucksack of 65-litre capacity is recommended to allow all the equipment to be carried easily. Footwear should consist of comfortable, soundly-made boots adequately treated with a waterproofing substance. If a winter traverse is considered crampons and an ice axe should be included. Long gaiters are necessary for winter conditions, as are thick woollen socks, thermal underwear, woollen breeches, shirt, pullover or fleece jacket, and a warm windproof outer garment. A waterproof jacket and trousers will be required for inclement weather. It should be remembered that wearing such clothing while ascending steep snow slopes, unroped, can greatly increase the speed of descent in the event of a fall or slip. A complete change of clothing is recommended for use at overnight stops after wet days. A good supply of socks for wearing with boots and with casual clothes is useful, as is a small container of detergent to enable you to wash clothes to be left overnight to dry. Youth hostels provide excellent drying facilities.

It is very important that participants can map-read and use a compass accurately. This is vital for precise navigation, especially in poor weather. It is strongly recommended that the four 1:25,000 scale Ordnance Survey Outdoor Leisure series maps covering the Lake District, and Harvey's walkers' maps, on which the maps in this book are based, are used to follow the walk accurately.

A compass and whistle for use in emergencies are essential. It is vital to carry a comprehensive first aid kit, including an elastic support bandage, in case of minor accidents, as well as a survival bag in case of emergencies involving an overnight stay on the fells. A water bottle, preferably of two-litre capacity, will certainly be necessary during the warm summer months. A good intake of liquid is required as a preventative measure against dehydration.

Participants may wish to record aspects of the walk, and a compact 35mm camera is handy. Small lightweight binoculars are also worthwhile for birdwatching and observing activity on the fell and in the valleys during rest breaks.

The list on the following page gives details of the items carried by the writer during the walk. While this list is fairly comprehensive, it is only a guide: some items may be excluded while others, for personal preference, are added.

Equipment taken by the author:

Bergan Model 557 frame rucksack
Boots: Dolomite Super Egger
Spare insoles for boots
Trainers and flip-flops
1 pair climbing breeches
1 pair jeans
4 shirts
3 pairs underwear
1 light pullover
4 pairs of walking socks
2 pairs of light casual socks
Gortex jacket
Gortex overtrousers
Cotton anklets
Cotton anorak
Hat with chin strap
2 pocket handkerchiefs
Pyjamas
Sleeping sheet
Survival bag
Leather belt pouch
Comprehensive first-aid kit

Toilet requisites: razor, soap, toothbrush, toothpaste, toilet paper, towel
Small plastic box repair kit containing: needle, thread, safety pins, tape
Plastic box containing: lens tissues, lens brush, filters, film, pen-type torch, glue, pencil, spare batteries
Water bottle (two-litre)
Small plastic bottle containing detergent for clothes
Small tin of leather oil for boots (Mars oil)
Head torch
Penknife
Maps (Ordnance Survey Outdoor Leisure Maps Nos 4, 5, 6 & 7, scale 1: 25 000) and map case
Pocket tape recorder plus 2 cassette tapes
Two cameras with associated lenses and monopod
Compact 8 x 20 binoculars
Compass and whistle
2 small notebooks; addresses/telephone numbers list
Money, Barclaycard, phonecard, Y.H.A. membership card
Sandwich box
Pocket-size bird identification book
Pocket-size edition of New Testament
Paperback reading book

Bibliography

The Cumbrian Way, J Trevelyan, Dalesman Publishing, 1987

The Lakeland Peaks, W A Poucher, Constable, 1983

Over Lakeland Fells, W A Poucher, Chapman & Hall, 1948

Fellwalking with Wainwright, A Wainwright, Michael Joseph, 1984

Wainwright's Coast to Coast Walk, A Wainwright, Michael Joseph, 1987

History Directory and Gazetteer and Directory of Cumberland and Westmorland, W Parson & W White, Republished by Michael Moon, 1976

National Trust Histories, The Lake District, C Baringer, William Collins, 1984

Wild Cumbria, W L Mitchell, Robert Hale, 1978

Mardale, The Drowned Village, David & Joan Hay, Friends of the Lake District, 1976

Two Thousand Miles of Wandering in the Border Country, Lakeland and Ribblesdale, Edmund Bogg, Leeds, & John Sampson, York, 1898

Heart of Lakeland – A Dalesman White Rose Guide, Dalesman Publishing, 1982

The King's England: Lake Counties, Cumberland & Westmorland, Arthur Mee, Hodder & Stoughton, 1937

Hamish's Mountain Walk, Hamish M Brown, Granada Publishing, 1980